Library of
Davidson College

The Future of Socialist Economic Integration

The Future of Socialist Economic Integration

Kálmán Pécsi
Edited with a Foreword by Paul Marer

M. E. Sharpe, Inc.
ARMONK, NEW YORK

Copyright © 1981 by M. E. Sharpe, Inc.
80 Business Park Drive, Armonk, New York 10504

All rights reserved. No part of this book may be reproduced in any form without written permission from the publisher.

Translated by George Hajdu and Keith Crane.

This book is a translation of *A KGST termelési integráció közgazdasági kérdései,* © Dr. Kálmán Pécsi, 1977. Originally published by Közgazdasági és Jogi Könyvkiadó, Budapest. This edition has been edited, revised and updated by the author.

Published simultaneously as Vol. XIX, no. 2-3, of *Eastern European Economics,* edited by Laura D'Andrea Tyson.

Library of Congress Cataloging in Publication Data

Pécsi, Kálmán.
    The future of socialist economic integration.

    Translation of an updated Hungarian revision of the 1977 ed. of the author's: A KGST termelési integráció közgazdasági kérdései.
    Published simultaneously as vol XIX, no. 2-3 of Eastern European economics.
    Bibliography: p.
    1. Council for Mutual Economic Assistance.
I. Marer, Paul. II. Title.
HC243.5.P4313   1981   337.47   81-2524
ISBN 0-87332-186-3   AACR2

Printed in the United States of America

Table of Contents

Foreword
  Paul Marer   vii

Preface to the U.S. Edition   xiii

Preface   xv

   I. The Process of Production Integration   3

   II. Specialization and Cooperation Projects
       in Production Integration   10

   III. Scientific and Technical Cooperation
        in Production Integration   40

   IV. The Role of International Economic Organizations
        and Joint Ventures in Production Integration   47

   V. New Methods of Production Integration:
       Target Programs   65

   VI. Regional Development and Production Integration   82

   VII. Pricing, Market, and Monetary Relations
        and Production Integration   88

   VIII. Problems of Trade Settled in Convertible
         Currencies among CMEA Member Countries   122

IX.	Efficiency and the Problem of Its Measurement in Production Integration	149
X.	The Influence of East-West Cooperation on CMEA Production Integration	161
	Notes	180
	Bibliography	186
	About the Author	189

Foreword
Paul Marer

This book is a milestone contribution by a leading Hungarian expert on economic integration among the socialist countries, that is, principally between the Soviet Union and Eastern Europe, under the auspices of the Council for Mutual Economic Assistance (the CMEA).

The CMEA is a regional institution established in 1949 to promote multilateral integration among its members.* During the 1950s the CMEA remained largely dormant, but during the 1960s and 1970s numerous attempts were made to transform it into an organization that would play a major role promoting regional economic integration among its members. Thus the CMEA's main objective is the same as that of the European Economic Community (EEC), which was founded in 1958 to pro-

---

*The USSR, Bulgaria, Czechoslovakia, Hungary, Poland, and Romania formed the CMEA in January 1949 (Albania joined about a month later but has taken no part in the CMEA's activities since 1961); the German Democratic Republic joined the CMEA in 1950, Mongolia in 1962, Cuba in 1972, and Vietnam in 1978.

Foreword

mote economic integration among the countries of Western Europe. To be sure, there are very important differences between the CMEA and the EEC. For example, the CMEA is not a supranational organization, while the EEC is one. Furthermore, while the principal mission of the EEC is to establish and referee the rules under which private enterprise can seek profitable commercial opportunities in the member countries, the CMEA's task is much more difficult: to find a mechanism of integration which can substitute for the market forces that are absent as long as its member's economies are strictly centrally planned.

This book is an "insider's" account of the CMEA's long search for a viable mechanism of integration. The account is partly historical and partly future oriented. It analyzes the achievements and shortcomings of various integration schemes that have been tried in the CMEA in the past and offers a set of recommendations for the future which, if implemented, would set the CMEA on a fundamentally different course than the direction it has been heading since it was established.

The author, Kálmán Pécsi, has excellent credentials: currently he is Chief of Department of Monetary and Commodity Relations of the CMEA Research Institute in Moscow, and his prior position was Head of Department on the Socialist Countries at the Institute of World Economics of the Hungarian Academy of Sciences in Budapest. This book is an updated and revised version of an earlier treatise published in Hungarian.

The timing of the book is fortuitous because the 1980s are likely to be a period of renewed interest in socialist economic integration. All CMEA countries are now seeking new sources of growth by improving the productivity of their economies; regional integration is one possible source that may be tapped for this purpose. The key question, explored in more comprehensive and specific terms here than in any other book published in Eastern Europe that I am aware of, is this: will the CMEA countries find, agree on, and be able to implement economic, trade, and financial arrangements for the region that will enhance the productivity of their economies and thus promote

Foreword

economic growth? Pécsi argues that because the economic environment of the 1980s will be very different from that of the 1960s and 1970s, it will not be possible for the CMEA countries simply to do more of the same of what they have been doing up to now. Among the circumstances that have changed, one of the most important is the likelihood that the Soviet Union will not be in a position to continue to supply a rapidly growing volume of energy and raw materials to Eastern Europe. The rapid expansion of Soviet exports of primary products to Eastern Europe during the last two decades was in large measure responsible for the integration achievements of the CMEA countries up to now. During the 1980s a new basis for integration will have to be found.

The economic environment of the 1980s will be more difficult for the CMEA countries, as also for much of the rest of the world, than was that of the 1960s or even the 1970s. This makes improved regional integration imperative but, at the same time, also more difficult. As this book so well documents, no consensus has yet been reached among the socialist countries regarding the basis on which specialization decisions should be made, how to measure and divide the benefits of specialization among the member countries, and — most important — what kind of regional trade, financial, and incentive systems would harmonize the interests of enterprises in different countries so that they would become willingly integrated, as suppliers and buyers, with firms in other CMEA countries.

The book deals in comprehensive fashion with many critical issues. On each issue the author first describes the situation as it has existed up to now, shows which of the traditional arrangements or practices have outlived their usefulness and why, and then offers a set of reform proposals. Pécsi provides much information and insight in a way that should be accessible even to nonspecialists; his analysis also contains much that will be new even to specialists on the topic, as suggested by the following sample of issues he explores:

— bilateral versus multilateral specialization agreements in

Foreword

the CMEA in finished products versus in parts and components, and what proportion of the agreements involves the phasing out of production of certain items versus simply endorsing earlier production decisions made independently by each CMEA country;
— a key aspect of regional economic integration is technology transfer. Pécsi describes CMEA agreements on research and development and contrasts the principles and practices of a free versus an adequately compensated flow of technical information among the member countries;
— discusses in considerable detail the much talked about CMEA "target programs," i.e., multilateral participation in investment projects located on the territory of one member country: how these projects differ from the more traditional forms of specialization, what key issues are debated in CMEA forums, and what are the main bottlenecks for implementation. Pécsi links the discussion of target programs to the broader issues of regional development and the economics of industrial location, focusing, for example, on the joint exploitation of Siberian energy and raw material resources by all CMEA countries;
— details old and new forms of financial relationships among the CMEA countries, calling attention to the growing importance of convertible-currency transactions in intra-CMEA trade. He also focuses on current obstacles to and future prospects for currency convertibility, analyzing whether it would be preferable to strive for the limited convertibility of the so-called transferable ruble or of that of the national currencies of the individual CMEA countries;
— explores the relationship between East-West trade, the growing convertible-currency indebtedness of the Eastern European countries, and CMEA integration. Pécsi argues that it is in the interest of both the Eastern and Western partners to improve the solvency of the CMEA countries and outlines ways in which this objective could be accomplished. (The discussion of this topic by a CMEA expert is of special interest and relevance today, given Poland's $24 billion in-

Foreword

debtedness to the West and that country's extremely serious external solvency problems.)

The basic proposition of Pécsi's book is that there are two competing integration models for the socialist countries. Under the first model — essentially relied on up to now — specialization decisions are made by the top planners in each country, who focus their efforts on the production of finished goods rather than of components and intermediate products and rely on plan coordination among the CMEA countries to implement decisions, with each country's planners giving administrative orders to enterprises under their jurisdiction. The alternative integration model is fundamentally different: integration decisions would be made principally by enterprises, prompted by economic and technical imperatives to establish long-term links with firms in other countries for the mutual delivery of intermediate products, parts, components, subassemblies, as well as of finished products. The incentive to specialize and the implementation of contracts would be guided by market signals, competition, and financial incentives. The introduction of this second model, in Pécsi's view, will require comprehensive domestic economic reforms in the CMEA countries and a substantial degree of "openness" vis-à-vis world commodity and financial markets. He argues that the CMEA countries sooner or later must adopt the second model if they expect to make significant further progress toward integration.

Having recently coedited a book on CMEA integration that summarizes the viewpoints of Western specialists on many of the same topics analyzed by Pécsi,* I had the occasion to reflect on the areas of agreement and disagreement between Pécsi's "inside" (though by no means consensus) views and Western "outside" perspectives on socialist integration. There is considerable common ground between Eastern and Western

---

*Paul Marer and J. M. Montias, eds., <u>East European Integration and East-West Trade</u> (Bloomington: Indiana University Press, 1980).

Foreword

specialists in identifying the shortcomings of CMEA integration. Pécsi, however, is much more specific when he presents and evaluates integration options available to the CMEA countries during the 1980s.

Bloomington, Indiana   Paul Marer
January 1981

Preface to the U.S. Edition

The earlier Hungarian edition of this book on CMEA production integration analyzed the period up to the beginning of 1978. Since then we have witnessed a number of expected as well as unforeseen developments in the world economy and in CMEA integration. Although in this version of the book I have updated wherever feasible the statistics and conclusions as of the beginning of 1980, I would like to call the reader's attention to two important developments concerning CMEA integration.

First, toward the end of 1978 and during 1979 there were theoretical and policy debates in the CMEA about the formation of prices in intra-CMEA trade, especially regarding the continued application of the moving average world market price method, discussed in Chapter VIII. After weighing carefully the advantages and shortcomings of alternative methods of price formation, at the beginning of 1980 it was decided to continue to use the moving average price method during the next five-year plan.

Second, in June 1980, according to official reports, the CMEA adopted very important recommendations, initiated principally by the USSR, regarding the expansion and deepening of manufacturing specialization. These initiatives represent the essence of the CMEA's integration policy during the 1981-85 plan period. This therefore means that — in contrast to the preceding plan

Preface to the U.S. Edition

period — the emphasis in solving the problem of energy and raw material supplies has now shifted from target programs to manufacturing specialization-cooperation.

I believe that these developments confirm the main conclusions of my book, namely, that (1) the further development of market and monetary relations, (2) the unification of production and market integration approaches, and (3) a significant move toward internal and external technological openness would contribute in a fundamental way to the further successful development of CMEA integration.

I would like to thank Messrs. Gyorgy Hajdu and Keith Crane and Professor Paul Marer for their help toward the publication of this book in the English language.

Budapest,   Kálmán Pécsi
August 1980

Preface

"Progress raises new problems. Widening the front of specialization and cooperation demands more exact control of the integration process, adaptation of production to the requirements of growing foreign economic relations, and the creation of new raw material and production complexes on a multilateral basis."

> From a speech by L. I. Brezhnev to the Eleventh Congress of the Hungarian Socialist Workers' Party.

Economic integration is successfully evolving in the Council for Mutual Economic Assistance. All the activities of the CMEA convincingly demonstrate what results participating countries can expect from these basically new methods of international economic relations grounded in the social ownership of the means of production, cooperation based on the principles of socialist internationalism, and respect for the sovereign rights and interests of every participating state.

The purpose of this book is, first of all, to analyze the problems of production integration, specialization, and cooperation, the activities of the international coordinating and economic or-

Preface

ganizations, target programs, technological and scientific cooperation, and the activities of joint enterprises in the spirit of the Comprehensive Program for the Extension and Strengthening of International Economic Specialization and Cooperation. These problems will also be analyzed in relation to monetary and fiscal problems and the development of a strategy of production integration. Throughout my analysis I will try to approach common, international interests from the Hungarian point of view. This approach provides for a better understanding of socialist integration and of the theoretical, practical, and economic policy motives of individual countries. The national positions taken on questions of general development can be understood only if we know these motives.

The book examines the importance of specialization and industrial cooperation, the development and successes of economic integration, and state and enterprise interests at both the micro and macro levels. I demonstrate the conditions necessary for the development of specialization and cooperation with respect to the international economic system (Chapters I and II).

In Chapter III I examine the problems of bilateral and multilateral cooperation and reimbursement in technical-economic cooperation, as well as increasing technical and scientific cooperation.

In the chapter on the problems of international economic organizations and joint enterprises (Chapter IV), I analyze the first stage of CMEA development, which began in 1962, and then the beginning of the present phase, its successes and problems.

I also look at the concept of cooperation in planning target programs, problems relating to the international flow of factors of production and its regional aspects, problems with calculating economic efficiency in the CMEA, monetary policies of individual countries, and trade and monetary relationships.

Production integration in the CMEA is not a closed process. CMEA integration is closely related to the rest of the world. The world economic developments that have occurred in the midseventies have also affected CMEA production integration. Hence the foreign economic environment must be taken into ac-

Preface

count in the integration of production.

During the implementation of so complicated and new a process as socialist integration, problems and difficulties may appear. The analysis of these problems is a weighty task. Yet we must undertake it, even if we cannot claim that no mistakes or errors have slipped into our analysis. It is only through such analytical work that we can explore those areas which make more rapid progress possible in this area.

June 1980

The Future
of Socialist
Economic Integration

Chapter I
The Process of Production Integration

1. The Present Level of Development of Production Integration

CMEA economic integration is proceeding at the tempo and in the general direction intended. Its tempo depends on the decisions of member countries, while the direction of integration is largely determined by initiatives for the solution of current and prospective economic problems of the socialist community.

In reviewing the progress of integration to date, we should note the motive force of the Soviet Union in pursuing this process.

The Soviet Union is the decisive factor in economic relations and integration among the CMEA countries. Cooperation with the Soviet Union is the chief guarantee for the smooth operation of production. This is due to its extensive market, great economic potential, and lesser dependence on foreign trade. The Soviet Union's position as raw material supplier and its vast market determine the structure of integration. In addition, political relations and bilateral economic relations with this country have a decisive impact on integration.

CMEA integration in the seventies differed considerably from that of the sixties. Multilateral approaches became of increasing importance in planning (mainly in coordinating investments); the CMEA countries are now actually implementing a number of

The Future of Socialist Economic Integration

joint investment projects. These developments in economic integration have been positive politically, at times more so than economically.

Recent changes in the international environment have been one of the driving forces of socialist economic integration. The disorders on the commodity and money markets in the West have forced all other countries and blocs to protect themselves from these conditions. These foreign disorders and certain domestic forces within the CMEA have made further integration of primary importance in terms of foreign policy, and they can be expected to lead to a new stage and new forms of integration during the eighties.

At this point we can only trace alternate plans for such changes. But we can surmise that their principal objective will probably be the further extension of economic integration. This would mean, for example, that economic policy will include coordination of planned capital and income transfers, the coordination and equalization of standard-of-living policies, a start on defining more clearly the geographic division of labor, and more consistent pricing methods among the individual countries.

These objectives form the outlines of the maximum foreseeable economic program of the eighties. When and to what extent they are adopted depend largely on the international environment and the international situation of the individual member countries. However, the main elements of this potential program are inherent in the successes of integration to date and in projects for the future.

We have now reached a stage at which the most important instrument of economic cooperation, i.e., cooperation in planning, has achieved tangible successes. The most important activity in this area is the coordination of long-term target programs. Through its initiatives the Soviet Union plays a decisive role in these programs. This can be seen in its ideas on how new sources of fuels and raw materials, which are principally located in Siberia and are thus quite remote from the European CMEA countries, can be developed jointly, and also how transport problems can be jointly solved.

The Process of Production Integration

Soviet researchers have kept one of the main problems of the member countries in sight when tracing the main outlines of specialization and cooperation in the CMEA: investment in machinery production. After the crystallization of common positions on fuels and raw materials, a more precise form for this type of cooperation will be the main area of planning integration. Up to this point the ideas under consideration have taken into account Soviet economic policy goals for increased exports of machinery and equipment and, also, the importance of increasing machinery exports from other member countries. Besides specialization in finished products, coordination can be found in an increasing number of agreements involving parts and components, mainly with economic regions in the European USSR.

The future location of industrial complexes is another important area for target planning. It is especially important to locate primary processing facilities close to raw material sources, of course, also taking labor force, capacity, infrastructure, and so on, into consideration.

The implementation of this model at a high level requires major simplifications in planning. No single country's plan can encompass the demands for the expanded production of resources. These problems will lead toward greater cooperation in planning at all levels. Ultimately cooperative planning in all sectors will be the only effective solution to these problems.

The second area of integration undergoing change is pricing. The question here is whether capitalist world market prices should continue to form the basis for CMEA prices or whether the domestic prices of the member countries should be the basis for prices in specialization and cooperation agreements. The latter alternative means a price structure in which prices can more easily become a channel for the redistribution of income. On the other hand, the world market price can reflect significant, worldwide changes in the relative efficiency of production. Since it is difficult to reconcile these two different functions, the debate on pricing will continue to be one of the knotty questions facing CMEA integration.

The Future of Socialist Economic Integration

After the adoption of the Comprehensive Program for CMEA integration, international economic organizations gained new impetus. As opposed to earlier experiences, these organizations should become bases for specialization in the coming years. International organizations should become control organs. They could create a common denominator for all those demands for which the partners had long been pressing to no avail within the framework of the usual CMEA procedures (e.g., more specialization, direct involvement of international organizations, different economic incentives, etc.). Despite this, production integration has problems in defining the functions of and launching joint ventures.

Little progress has been made on the issue of the convertibility of the transferable ruble. In view of the emphasis on production integration, transferability has been of only limited importance, and no change should be expected for a long while. However, the situation is different in the case of nonmember countries wanting to join the transferable ruble bloc. There is every indication that some form of transferability must be created for them, primarily for political reasons. Transferability developed on such a basis will probably also have an effect on transferable ruble transactions among member countries.

In the near future there may be a substantial change in the gold content of the transferable ruble. New exchange rates for convertible currencies are important for the formation of transferable ruble prices in the short run. This step could have a significant effect on exchange rate policies among the member countries over the long term as well.

In recent years the institutional framework for intergovernmental direction of integration has been expanded to include the Planning Cooperation Committee (PCC). The importance of this organ has grown steadily since its creation. Developments to date show that practically parallel "jurisdiction" has developed between the PCC and other CMEA organs and standing committees. In spite of all its other negative aspects, this circumstance has the advantage that a "two channel" approach can be adapted to certain questions in the CMEA. In certain cases this would allow greater flexibility in negotiations (although it also calls for more careful coordination within the individual countries).

These phenomena draw attention to the fact that the establishment of an apparatus and institutions for the control of integration is far from complete. More effective control and supervision will probably only gain greater importance with more joint planning and even then will depend on the actual methods used for integration.

If the environment evolves suitably, a new important stage of integration will commence in the eighties. It will be based on assured long-term agreements on raw materials, further specialization and cooperation, and agreements on pricing.

2. Production Integration in the General Theory of Integration

Socialist economic integration is a historical process. Its purpose is to create an efficient form of regional integration that includes the amalgamation of national markets, the emergence of a large, integrated economic community, and the ensuing consequences with respect to political superstructures: ultimately, through economic union or some other form of integration, nations will become roughly equal. But this lies far in the future.

The socialist model of integration has two aspects: production integration and market integration.

In the process of production integration, the macrolevel production problems of the national economies are of primary importance. The objective is to develop efficient national economic structures and to link production processes through specialization and cooperation. Optimal national economic structures develop through expanding production relationships, and this raises the problem of technological standardization in the cooperating countries.

In the process of market integration, markets are amalga-

The Future of Socialist Economic Integration

mated. Trade barriers are abolished, and commodities are sold in a fixed institutional framework. Ultimately this means that the financial system plays an active role. Included here are such factors as the existence of market and monetary instruments (each having uniform purchasing power) suitable for measuring efficiency, the flow of factors of production, and other elements closely related to money. All this assumes direct relationships between producers and enterprises.

I have divided the single integration process in two in order to show differences between levels of development of production and market integration. Production integration cannot be implemented without market integration. However, the two types of integration can occur at different tempos.

Until now, on the basis of the Comprehensive Program, prominence has been given to production integration, while market integration has been forced into the background. And up to now production integration has been characterized by extensive growth. Its main task has been the planned organization and expansion of production cooperation and increased specialization.

The principal instrument of production integration is the coordination of plans. Basically, the coordinated plan for integration entails a program for the distribution of raw materials, machinery, technology, and manpower needed for the target programs and the distribution of output listed in material balances. Actual integration is achieved through joint individual production activities. No uniform monetary, social, or employment policy has been developed. Furthermore, production integration and production planning must take into account the fact that large-scale structural transformations planned on the central level require large investments in each country.

Further progress in this extensive production integration model means that the establishment of closer communitywide cooperation will remain unlikely, as will the subsequent establishment of a uniform industrial base. In the extensive production integration model, the member countries look out for their own interests primarily within the framework of bilateral cooperation with the individual members and with countries outside the community.

At present a special role in integration is assigned to developing sources of raw materials and energy and the necessary infrastructure called for by the target programs. Even if levels of participation in proportion to the capacity of the individual countries are adopted rather than the present proposals, which appear excessive, there will be no change in the role of countries in these programs. Thus the problem of raw materials and energy and the provision of the necessary infrastructure for their development will remain the basic issue of cooperation.

Economic processes influence when and how far any theory is able to withstand rational criticism. This holds true for production integration as well, and it leads to a question: Is it sufficient merely to make extensive use of resources, or should we not, on the CMEA level, make use of potential reserves arising from intensive economic methods and the unification of production and market integration? This is the question posed by this book.

Chapter II
Specialization and Cooperation Projects in Production Integration

1. The Concept of International Specialization and Cooperation

The CMEA document "Principles of the Socialist International Division of Labor," adopted in the early sixties, defines the concept of production specialization and cooperation as follows:

> Specialization among states means that the production of the same kinds of products to satisfy the needs of all the interested countries is concentrated in one or a few socialist countries. In this context the standards of production technology and organization are raised, and stable economic relations and production cooperation are established among the countries. The result of international specialization in production is that production volume increases, costs are reduced, labor productivity rises, product quality improves, and the technical features of the products are perfected.

This rather general definition must be broken down in detail both for international specialization and for cooperation.

International production specialization has become rather generally defined as: permanent division of the production (and development) of finished products, main units, or parts between

Specialization and Cooperation Projects

individual countries — or their economic units — with the aim of satisfying needs under more efficient conditions by increasing the scale of production and by concentrating and shortening development efforts.

Specialization has occurred up to now mainly on the basis of recommendations by CMEA organs or the resolutions of bilateral technical and scientific cooperation commissions. The definition thus stresses the governmental nature of international specializations.

Recently, however — at least among Hungarian economists — the view has emerged that the extent of production specialization is not determined by its legal forms but by its economic content and substance. Accordingly, one should consider as international specialization not only the recommendations of CMEA organs, resolutions adopted by bilateral commissions, and relations based on contracts for production specialization and cooperation, but also the permanent foreign trade agreements that affect the volume, efficiency, and distribution of output. Hence product concentration through foreign trade can be regarded as a kind of centrally implemented specialization as a result of international specialization. Such a specialization process has had an important impact on the structure of Hungarian industry, particularly in engineering (e.g., in shipbuilding, the production of motor vehicles, etc.).

Production cooperation can be defined as a permanent relationship between producers that is based on the conscious and preplanned joint activity of legally independent economic organizations, and whose objective is to divide the production of certain parts or major units of some finished product in the interest of a rational utilization of productive capacities, an increase in production scales, and rational management of investment funds. Such cooperation agreements among enterprises may also include sharing designs and construction, sales, parts supply, joint establishment of service networks, and so on.

Thus this definition of the concept of cooperation stresses direct relations between producers and the role of the legally independent economic organizations. Such cooperation has eco-

The Future of Socialist Economic Integration

nomic properties that permit us to distinguish it from specialization between countries.

Up to now production cooperation in parts, subassemblies, and technology through direct interenterprise relations has rarely been undertaken by socialist countries. It is an area in which specialization and cooperation have been most unsatisfactory and which holds the greatest room for expansion. Implementation of such cooperation between enterprises demands the solution of much more complex economic problems than specialization between countries. Problems related to pricing and market relations that affect the interests of enterprises are of primary importance.

In short, production integration among the CMEA countries can be attained in two major ways:

The first, specialization between countries, includes mainly specialization agreements initiated by the main CMEA organs and the central organs of the individual countries. Specialization in international trade revealed in product concentration belongs in this category. Up to now this form of production integration has predominated among the CMEA countries.

The other is cooperation based on enterprise interests. It relies mainly on direct contacts between enterprises and implies division of the production of subassemblies, parts, joint establishment of technological development, sales, parts supply, and the like. Up to now this form has not shown particular progress among the CMEA countries.

2. The Development and Results of Specialization

Deliberate attempts at production specialization within the CMEA framework began in the second half of the 1950s. For a long time the view prevailed in the CMEA organs that international specialization implies a division of products among countries established on the basis of recommendations by CMEA organs or resolutions by bilateral commissions; under this framework the given product is produced by one country, while

Specialization and Cooperation Projects

the others do not produce it. The country specializing in the product acts to satisfy the total demand of countries that do not produce it.

According to this concept the main mode of specialization was the recommendations for specialization in various products. Such recommendations were first made in the CMEA in 1956. They included a wide range of products. Between 1956 and 1972 in the engineering industry alone, about 5,300 recommendations were made for specialization, cooperation, and mutual deliveries. By 1975, 35 multilateral international production specialization agreements had been signed.[1] Of them 20 were made in engineering, four in radio technology, five in the chemical industry, one in nonferrous metallurgy, one in nuclear energy, one in agriculture, and one in air traffic. Between 1972 and 1977, 101 such agreements were signed. Hungary took part in 84 of them. Bilateral production specialization agreements are also widespread: their number lies between 650 and 700; and Hungary participates in 129 of them.

As a result of international agreements on production specialization, the production of several industrial products is concentrated in a few countries. Thus, e.g., of the 1,927 products included in the 20 agreements on production specialization in engineering, 876 items (45.6%) are produced in a single country, 547 (28.4%) in two countries, and 499 items (25.8%) are concentrated in three countries. Thus about 99% of the engineering products covered by the 20 agreements are produced in, at most, three countries.

Characteristically, specialization in finished products now predominates. Specialization is less widespread in parts and components, certain technological processes, or groups of products. Only two agreements covering 371 items provide for specialization in parts among the 20 multilateral production specialization agreements in engineering that cover 1,927 products.

As a result of proposals on production specialization and cooperation and the concentration of production that stem from the agreements concluded there was a somewhat reduced tendency in some branches of engineering for countries to start producing articles already produced by the others. However, under the 20 engineering agreements mentioned, only in 44 cases do we find countries intending to phase out production lines duplicated in some other country. At the same time, 122 cases can be found that initiate the production of certain products already being produced in other CMEA countries. This indicates that the individual countries have not yet sufficiently coordinated their long-term development programs for the industries affected.

It would be almost impossible to compare the results of specialization among countries with the volume of cooperation based on enterprise interests. As has been said, cooperation relying on enterprise interests is very infrequent, not only between Hungary and the other CMEA countries, but also among the latter.

Why are the results of specialization initiated by central decision-makers more substantial than those of cooperation implemented by reliance on enterprise interests? The reasons are clear. The real needs of the countries in physical terms, based on internal product balances, are specified in long-term and annual foreign trade agreements. These agreements reflect real needs, while in cooperation implemented on the basis of enterprise interests, increased productivity and profitability are the basic motives. Up to now, however, they have been of lesser importance than the former factor. Thus until now specialization agreements established and implemented on the basis of central directives laid down in trade agreements have proved firmer bases for the development of specialization.

Such specialization agreements are generally established among countries, and state organs take responsibility for their implementation. Thus it is largely irrelevant that since January 1, 1968, in Hungary, proposing and carrying out such specialization have been placed within the enterprises' discretion (or if an obligation was assumed by higher organs, the enterprise could decide for itself whether to participate in the specialization). What is relevant here is that for countries with directive planning systems — hence for Hungary's partners —

Specialization and Cooperation Projects

such specialization better fits their plans and their planning of production of and trade in machinery and equipment. Specialization at the governmental level allows the exporting country to determine what it wants to produce, and for the importer it secures needed machines from a reliable source through specialization agreements.

At the same time, we should not forget that although the specialization "among countries" set up in foreign trade agreements is greater in volume, it is neither complete nor comprehensive. The problems arising from differing interests, price systems, positions of enterprises, technological standards, etc., are also present in trade transacted on the basis of such specialization. Preliminary profitability computations are very unreliable both conceptually and numerically. And profitability and efficiency have been pushed into the background due to the system of direct economic control.

Coordination of plans is an important condition for developing specialization. In spite of the successes attained, we cannot be satisfied here. One of the main reasons is that in highly important fields of the economy, even the countries affected had in several cases no clear long-term development goals. Yet such goals are undoubtedly a necessary condition for harmonizing plans and carrying out specialization. Only when they exist can it be hoped that countries will not merely harmonize current plans that at most take into account shorter- and medium-term conditions but also clarify the longer-run perspectives. For example, in order to satisfactorily set the optimal size of some investments or to decide whether to develop or curtail a whole industry, as well as to resolve specialization issues, it is necessary to know the long-term plans of cooperating countries.

Summing up, we can say that at the present level of development of production in CMEA countries, the available opportunities for production integration are certainly not used adequately. The reasons for this state of affairs can be summed up roughly as follows. First, agreements on specialization and cooperation have not always established the most efficient division of labor for the whole CMEA. Second, the agreements were adopted for organizational, economic, and other reasons relating more to existing conditions of integration and the level of cooperation than to the requirements of intensifying integration. Third, the agreements have not promoted division of labor in the selected sectors; rather, they were directed at strengthening the existing industries in the member countries, which were taken as inviolable, and at creating similar industries in the less developed member countries, instead of apportioning industries among the countries of the region.

3. The Development of Motor Vehicle Production in Hungary: A Successful Example of CMEA Specialization

In this section I will analyze a successful case of CMEA production integration. My investigation encompasses two points. I first examine the issues and ensuing proposals and measures designed to resolve them in order to determine how similarly successful cooperations might be initiated in order to promote better adaptation of the national economies of CMEA member countries to each other.

Second, I examine the level of integration and the potentials of the given stage of development. Thus I assume that we are now in an extensive stage of production integration; the only realistic approach is one that does not confuse the development stages of integration and does not attempt to prescribe solutions impracticable at this stage.

Development of motor vehicle production was a priority government program in Hungary under the Fourth Five-Year Plan. Today this industry contributes one fourth of the output of the engineering industry and almost one third of its exports. Production of motor vehicles directly employs 45,000 to 50,000 people and indirectly entails the employment of many more. It is thus important to note that the requirements of CMEA specialization in conveyance motor vehicle production hinged on a national economic development strategy.

The major enterprises participating in the program — Ikarus,

Specialization and Cooperation Projects

the Csepel Auto Works, the Raba Hungarian Railway Carriage and Machine Works, the Electric Auto Equipment Works, and so on — have almost tripled their output in the last five years. This large and growing role of motor vehicle production was made possible by integration through the CMEA. Building vehicles and producing parts is profitable only in very large series. The necessary conditions for such production were provided by the cooperation accord set up by the CMEA countries.

During the Fourth Five-Year Plan, Ikarus turned out about 41,000 buses, and it plans to produce more than 60,000 during the Fifth Plan period. In 1979 output was about 13,600 units; in 1980 it will be 13,800 units. Of these 9,500 were exported to other CMEA countries in 1979, and 9,700 will be in 1980. The factory thus produces on a competitive scale in Europe, as can be seen from the data in Tables 1 and 2.

The main market for buses is the USSR and the German Democratic Republic. For example, in 1976 we delivered 6,000 buses to the Soviet Union and sent them a further 700 as an investment contribution to building the Orenburg gas pipeline. We sold more than 1,400 buses to the GDR and 650 to other CMEA countries. About 1,300 units went to capitalist countries, and 1,600 were retained for domestic use.

Under specialization agreements products from other socialist countries are also used in the production of buses. For example, the USSR supplies front axles for large buses. Eight-and-a-half-meter buses are produced with parts supplied by the GDR. Rear axles are produced in large series by the Raba Works in Györ, which supplies not only the Ikarus factory but also the motor vehicle industries of other CMEA countries. Györ's output of rear axles increased from 211,000 units under the Fourth Five-Year Plan to 340,000 under the Fifth. In 1975 more than 27,000 unites were delivered to the Soviet Union, 6,000 to Poland, 2,700 to Czechoslovakia, and 500 to Bulgaria. A considerable portion of the Györ work's output is also exported under cooperation agreements.

Under the division of labor established with the GDR, various electrical devices for cars, axles for agricultural equipment,

Table 1

Bus Production by Selected European Firms in 1974

Country	Firm	Production Units
France	Berliet	1,490
	Saviem	2,219
Federal Republic of Germany	Mercedes	13,726
	Kass Bohrer	1,152
	Magirus Deutz	1,508
	MAN	1,607
Italy	Fiat	4,832
	Om	3,604
Sweden	Volvo Scania	3,889
United Kingdom	B. Leyland Bedford	33,667
Hungary	Ikarus	8,000

Table 2

European Bus Production in 1978

Country	Output	Export
Hungary (1979)	13,600	more than 9,500
France	3,683	400
FRG	14,585	8,230
Italy	5,308	1,313
Sweden	4,744	4,084
United Kingdom	23,005	10,485
Spain	2,873	1,364

Specialization and Cooperation Projects

etc., are supplied to the GDR vehicle industries. At the same time, we get from them axles for buses, driver seats, and heating equipment. We also have specialization agreements with the Czechoslovak vehicle industry. We supply Bulgaria with partial assemblies for certain kinds of buses. Since 1976 we have supplied, in addition to rear axles and motors, hydraulic springs, steering wheels, and transmissions for Bulgarian buses. In 1980 at least 360 partial assemblies for buses will be delivered by Mogürt. In return we get from our Bulgarian partners vehicle parts, lifts, and fittings for buses.

In 1976 experimental series production of parts for hydraulic transmissions for the USSR was begun. According to the agreements, in 1980, 8,000 assemblies and in 1985, 20,000 assemblies consisting of 36 units each will be supplied. The USSR in return will meet Ikarus needs for complete gearboxes.

Broad cooperation has also evolved in the production of various parts for cars. Best known is the Zhiguli agreement, under which various assemblies, parts, complete instrument panels, windshield wipers, ignition switches, locks, door handles, radios, and so on, are supplied to the Volga Car Factory. Similar cooperation has also developed in the production of the Polski Fiat and Moskvich cars.

Almost 80,000 cars were imported in 1976 from the CMEA countries for Hungarian needs. Of them more than 30,000 came from the USSR, the same number from the GDR, 10,000 from Czechoslovakia, 5,000 from Poland, and 1,000 from Romania. Specialization in parts for cars permits us to counterbalance about half of our car imports from the USSR and Poland with parts produced under specialization-cooperation agreements.

Cooperation also extends to trucks. Partial assemblies are shipped to the new Kama Truck Factory for the Kamaz. For example, in 1976 we supplied 8,000 pairs of low- and high-pitch horns; we will export 50,000 in 1980. Under the Hungarian-Romanian agreement for the production of heavy trucks, engines are supplied by the Györ factory. Relying on Romanian, Bulgarian, and Polish orders, the production of power steering units will double at the Csepel Car Factory, thus helping meet the demand for trucks in the CMEA countries. In 1976 we imported more than 14,000 trucks, mainly from the GDR and the USSR but also partly from the ČSSR and Romania.

In most cases cooperation with the CMEA countries has also facilitated profitable exports to the West. Production specialization based on exploiting the advantages inherent in the socialist international division of labor makes our products — engines, axles, and buses — competitive on capitalist markets as well, since they are produced in a modern way and in large series. Thus their quality standards and technical parameters are also competitive. Interest on the part of the advanced capitalist countries in purchasing and marketing our products is growing (e.g., Volvo and two major U.S. companies). Since the products of the capitalist partners set world standards, products turned out in cooperation with socialist countries have to meet the highest quality standards. Both effects influence the Hungarian enterprises participating in specialization: they are constantly and increasingly compelled to observe and maintain quality standards. It should be mentioned here that some materials, parts, and units for Ikarus buses were imported for quite a while from Western European countries with developed industries. For example, the laminated windshields of buses capable of 100 kilometers per hour came from Finland; shock absorbers came from England and Italy; the sound and heat baffles, outer finishing materials, and polyurethane for the seats came from the Federal Republic of Germany. In some cases this is still the case. Usually, however, the Hungarian enterprises purchased licenses that met standards for buses from Western countries (e.g., electropneumatic equipment for operating doors, shock absorbers, gearboxes, finishing paints, heat and sound insulating materials, etc.), and today they meet the needs of the bus industry with high-quality domestic production.

It should be quite clear that specialization in the production of motor vehicles is a good example of the advantages of socialist economic integration, particularly production integration. Relying on the CMEA division of labor and on increasing

Specialization and Cooperation Projects

international specialization and production integration, mass production, technological modernization, and meeting quality requirements have generally promoted higher quality standards. Specialization in the production of motor vehicles shows that in order to get the funds needed to steadily raise technological standards, we need not only those markets where the commodity produced will mainly be used but third markets as well in order to exploit the advantages of socialist economic integration to the fullest.

All this also shows that specialization based on the socialist international division of labor does not and cannot lead to isolation. On the contrary, it can increase East-West cooperation: CMEA specialization lets us exploit the advantages to be derived from large-scale production, but world market pressures are also needed to constantly raise quality standards. In the process of East-West cooperation this leads to increased exports to capitalist countries and thus to improving quality standards, thereby contributing to the satisfaction of the needs of the CMEA countries for ever-increasing quality.

The following major conclusions can be drawn from the Hungarian case. First, that for a specialization project to successfully change the economic structure of a country, it must originate from the national economic plan of the given country and from its internal needs. The motor vehicle project is one of the few priority development programs in Hungary. Second, to succeed in penetrating foreign markets and to coordinate technological modernization there must be a rational blend in the given country between specializations in the production of parts and of finished products. Individual parts and assemblies have to be produced for several markets. At the same time, each country should also produce finished goods in addition to parts.

There are, however, other lessons that are more general. For instance, at some point parts and plants must be replaced or remodeled. Diversification of production and a lengthening list of articles produced mean that research, planning, design, and technological development must also meet the requirements of modernity. High productivity and high levels of technology can be attained only if production volume permits the use of efficient equipment, automated machines, modern technologies, and modern forms of production organization. The minimum level of production below which it is unprofitable to produce exceeds the domestic needs of some countries in several industries. Thus setting the optimum scale of production and size of enterprises is perhaps the most important factor promoting rational allocation of production. In short, the tendency toward production concentration inevitably leads to the international division of labor. If we neglect this aspect, we are heading toward continuing uneconomic production.

4. Relations between the Process of Specialization and Machinery Imports

The relationship between the process of specialization and the importation of machinery is of great interest with regard to machinery production and imports of machinery in the CMEA. Our analysis will concern only Bulgaria, Hungary, Poland, and Romania. Statistics from these four countries can provide some insights on specialization in the machine industry. Soviet statistics on machinery production and imports have been omitted because Soviet specialization and investment in machinery depend mainly on their domestic market.

Imports from the member countries play a very small part in USSR investments in machinery and equipment. Czechoslovakia and the GDR were omitted because they both produce on their own about 60 to 80% of the articles found in the world nomenclature of engineering products, and thus they are basically self-sufficient. A quite separate issue is the fact that this is not a natural state of affairs but the result of problems in the various economic systems; it reveals some inefficiencies in CMEA specialization because duplicate capacities were developed.

Between 1955 and 1975 the shares of domestic and imported machinery in total investments in machinery by the CMEA

Specialization and Cooperation Projects

countries examined differed substantially. Hungary has probably headed most steadily toward "opening" its economy, while in investment and development in Poland and Romania, the shares of domestically produced machines and equipment show identical ratios over a long period. Thus the results of specialization within the CMEA are not very satisfactory from the import side.

Another major conclusion is that within total imports of machinery and equipment from CMEA countries and the USSR, the ratio of imports was almost constant up to 1970; but while in Poland the share of the Soviet Union increased, in Hungary and Bulgaria it declined somewhat, and it fell sharply in Romania. After 1970, however, the ratio fell markedly in Poland and stabilized in Bulgaria and Hungary.

In spite of the fact that the leading CMEA organs always stress growing cooperation and specialization among CMEA countries, the process does not appear to have expanded when we examine it over a long period of time. Thus specialization and cooperation on the macroeconomic level need to be improved.

Finally, the data also reflect the rather surprising fact that the ratio of CMEA imports in total imports of machinery and equipment is stable both for Bulgaria and Hungary. The situation is different for Romania, but the whole development of Romanian foreign trade differs from that of the other member countries. During the seventies Polish machinery imports from the CMEA also considerably declined.

I also examined annual changes in the share of investment in machinery and equipment from imports in the CMEA countries and their relation to changes in total investments in machinery and equipment (see Table 3). The data suggest that in the countries that were initially less developed — Bulgaria and Romania — the share of domestic production increased, with a corresponding decrease in imports. This occurred while total investment expanded. In Hungary import growth is obvious, showing that the country is becoming more "open"; moreover, differences between the annual rates of investments and the

Table 3

Total Investments and Sources of Machinery and
Equipment Imports for Four CMEA Countries

Year	Total value of investment	Of which		Among imports	
		domestic production, %	imports, %	from the CMEA, %	from the Soviet Union, %
		Bulgaria (million leva)			
1955	168.1	43.5	56.5	83.2	42.3
1960	355.2	47.8	62.2	91.8	53.4
1965	649.1	39.0	61.0	81.9	53.1
1970	1,209.9	48.0	52.0	79.9	48.8
1974	1,692.7	46.0	54.0	84.0	52.2
1978	2,561.0	56.0	44.0	86.0	57.0
		Hungary (billion forint)			
1958	8.4	66.7	33.3	76.5	20.4
1960	17.3	49.5	59.5	81.1	35.5
1965	18.6	57.0	43.0	79.6	39.5
1970	35.7	50.3	49.7	76.5	28.9
1974	52.6	47.2	52.8	75.2	32.0
1978	80.7	53.0	47.0	56.0	21.0

Poland
(billion zloty)

Year					
1960	31.9	70.7	29.3	73.3	30.0
1965	53.7	72.1	27.9	81.4	33.8
1970	82.1	71.3	28.7	78.2	37.3
1975	240.0	n.a.	n.a.	53.1	23.5
1978	293.5	81.0	19.0	61.0	27.5

Romania
(billion lei)

Year					
1955	4.3	74.5	25.5	95.4	67.3
1960	8.8	77.3	22.7	73.0	27.8
1965	17.6	71.3	28.7	62.1	19.2
1970	32.4	72.5	27.5	54.5	13.9
1974	54.1	75.8	24.2	n.a.	n.a.
1978	95.0	84.0	16.0	n.a.	21.0

Sources: National statistical yearbooks.

growth of imports are evident. It can be seen from the data that the industrialization policy pursued in the fifties and sixties led in practically every country to unilateral development of their own engineering industries, and the trend continues. This policy of import substitution has led the majority of CMEA countries to a decreasing dependence of their investment on imports (at least as regards imports from member countries).

Increased specialization should help stop this trend, although one cannot expect the current process to take a radical turn.

In the interest of greater efficiency, it would also be expedient to largely "merge" the engineering industries of the GDR and Czechoslovakia on the basis of specialization. In the USSR solutions to the problems of internal specialization call for major efforts. In short, our main conclusion is that in the extensive model of production integration, if no measures are taken against policies of import substitution, a decreasing dependence on imports ensues, countries duplicate each others' product lines, and economic efficiency in the CMEA decreases. Only by a transition to the intensive model, by "opening up" the economies and increasing specialization among the countries, can this situation be remedied.

5. The Problem of Quality in the Specialization Process

Adopting the alternative of a technological "opening up," as opposed to import substitution, is most often blocked in the specialization process by the fact that quality considerations have, until quite recently, been pushed into the background. This affects both specialization and cooperation. Studies on the subject disclosed, e.g., that at the end of the sixties, 47% of the industrial articles were below world standards. Even in Czechoslovakia — which is the most advanced of the CMEA countries and most quality oriented — at the end of the sixties, 61% of engineering products did not meet world standards.[2] In the Soviet engineering industry the share of highest quality goods

Specialization and Cooperation Projects

is still negligible, while the bulk consists of lower-quality and substandard products. This is shown for 1973 by the data in Table 4. More recent data are not available, but in my view the situation has not changed fundamentally as of 1980.

Low-quality goods have high social costs. The same resources can be used to produce either a large quantity of low-quality commodities or to put out an adequate volume of high-quality articles. In order to maintain a high rate of growth, in every CMEA country an extensive economic policy was pursued whereby a growing part of national income was used for investment. In this situation increases in living standards had to be achieved through quality improvements. But in the CMEA countries a sellers' market still dominates; enterprises can sell low-quality goods without any major difficulty. This makes the goal of improved quality difficult to achieve.

Due to the existence of a sellers' market, specialization in end products is not enough to ensure improved quality. If specialization in end products is achieved, quality demands are not

Table 4

Distribution of Engineering Products by Quality Categories in 1973, in %

	Highest category	Categories		Classified as substandard products
		I	II	
Total engineering of which:	3.5	46.2	1.5	48.8
heavy machinery	11.4	58.9	1.0	28.7
machine tools	2.8	68.8	3.6	24.7
agricultural machinery	7.4	44.0	0.5	48.1

Source: <u>Investitsionnye problemy narodnokhoziaistvennykh kompleksov</u>, Moscow, "Nauka" Publishers, 1975, p. 83.

stressed. Should the quality of a machine obtained from a partner who specializes in it not be adequate, it will perhaps not be put into operation, or no more similar machines will be ordered. But if we assemble parts and units in a cooperation process, consistent high quality has an importance that reaches across borders. This is convincingly shown by the case of a Hungarian firm participating in the Zhiguli cooperation that thanks to quality problems, had to order parts from a capitalist partner in order to meet the needs of the Soviet enterprise. When we specialize in parts or technological processes, greater efficiency can be assured only if the parts can be assembled.

The other aspect of the problem is that "he who produces better should fare better." Competition cannot be dispensed with when we expand cooperation.

Solving the quality problems and reaching world standards are possible only by shifting from an extensive to an intensive mode of production. This implies the opening up of trade, the convertibility of currency, and the establishment of competition among enterprises, all of which will necessitate the adoption of quality-improving methods in other countries. Moreover, the influence of demanding world market standards in trade will also lead to higher quality. Thus quality problems can be solved through the process of specialization.

6. Harmonizing Objectives in the Development of Engineering and Specialization

The scientific and technical revolution and intensive economic development demand the qualitative development of the engineering industry in every member country. This has been recognized by the countries themselves. The structural change implemented in the individual countries and the modifications of development concepts testify to this effect. Because of differences in scale and other factors, problems vary by countries; but some of them are common to every CMEA country. They are the following:

Specialization and Cooperation Projects

— the supply of primary materials to the engineering industries has to be improved, and the use of modern chemical products has to be increased;

— it is necessary to reduce or eliminate the production of obsolescent items;[3]

— product quality must be improved, and the technical standards set for them must be raised.

In the last two decades engineering production also considerably affected the growth of national income in the member countries. Despite its active role in industrialization and in various structural changes, it claimed a relatively modest share of total investment. The view is rather widespread in the CMEA countries that because of its relatively low capital intensity, the relative ease of internal structural changes, its short gestation periods, and its flexibility, the profitability of engineering is sure to remain above average in the long run as well.[4] This conclusion also seems to be supported by the consistent efforts of the industrial and foreign trade organs of the CMEA countries to attain ever higher exports of engineering products.

But in the present extensive stage of production integration in the CMEA there are a number of new factors whose neglect may entail unfavorable consequences. Thus, e.g., opportunities for the domestic use or export of obsolete equipment are fading, and this considerably reduces the profitability of sales.

The earlier low investment ratios of engineering were dictated by national priorities. Up to a point this had an adverse effect on quality, while the elimination of obsolescence on a massive scale already claims a large portion of national resources.

Since the CMEA countries have attained approximately equal levels of development, and because of the requirements of its own internal development, the behavior of the largest CMEA machinery importer, i.e., of the USSR, is going to change. It seems that at least a part of the economic press and some practical experts have failed as yet to draw the ensuing conclusions.

While the share in the economy of socialist engineering in-

The Future of Socialist Economic Integration

dustries has attained or now approximates similar indicators in industrially advanced countries, the CMEA countries will not be prepared to completely supply their national economies with modern equipment for five to ten years. In every CMEA country the system of incentives stimulates much more the raising of productivity and improving cost and profitability indicators than the massive release of products turned out with up-to-date technologies and pioneering performance. The CMEA countries have chosen as the best solution to this problem — besides increasing their own research and development efforts — the producing of licenses, technologies, whole factories, and high-performance automated equipment from industrially advanced capitalist countries, and to a lesser extent, the establishment of production cooperation with capitalist firms. But we see only traces of incorporating East-West technological cooperation into long-term organized international economic cooperation within the CMEA. We have not yet exploited the advantages that could be derived from the combined cooperation of several CMEA countries in large technical and production projects with major Western firms on the forefront of the engineering industry. Indeed, apart from the USSR, no single CMEA country is an adequate partner for them.

Changes in recent years have worked toward expanding international specialization in production. This is shown by the number of agreements concluded on specialization. But a major structural intertwining of the CMEA countries' engineering industries has not yet occurred. Furthermore there is still excess production in the CMEA of some obsolete machines, equipment, and product groups. On the other hand, there is a chronic shortage of modern engineering products. This situation cannot be attributed merely to the methods used in international cooperation. One must look for its causes in the fact that there is no long-term program for the division of labor in the engineering industry that encompasses the whole socialist world economy.

Related to this problem is the fact that duplication of investment exists among the countries of the CMEA, and that almost

Specialization and Cooperation Projects

equal pressure is exerted by the demand for new plants as by the demand for modernizing old plants. Limited investment resources and poor quality make it difficult to modernize all the processes involved in producing a product. Thus the more advanced the level of industrialization, the greater the danger that investments might become fragmented. In investment the choice between various industries and that between expansion and modernization cause constant dilemmas. All this easily leads to overinvestment and, simultaneously, to a decline in the productivity of capital.

Because of these problems the CMEA countries have difficulties selling the products of certain industries. Export drives duplicate each other: competing, not complementary products are exported to foreign markets. Since these products are generally produced by large industries in which substantial investments have been made, specialization can take place only slowly. At the same time, since neither the quality of the products nor their production costs meet world market standards, specialization makes sense only if it is linked to modernization. Without it the huge investments entailed in specialization would never be returned. Further development of the existing capital goods industries is hindered by the fact that the products can be exported for hard currencies only with growing difficulty. Specialization demands so much investment that in the present economic situation, characterized as it is by low capital productivity, these investments would draw resources from the operation of existing plants. This is why efficient investment is emphasized in the foreign economic policy of the member countries.

There are several engineering reasons that make progress in specialization difficult, especially in subassemblies and production cooperation, areas in which the Twenty-eighth Session of the CMEA Council found the pace of development too slow. For example, in the CMEA countries there are few factories that could expressly specialize in subassemblies. Also, the international standardization of subassemblies and parts is on a low level. It is difficult to establish direct production relations between enterprises. The material interests of the coop-

The Future of Socialist Economic Integration

erating parties and the anticipated results of the cooperation are difficult to quantify. Various erroneous approaches also play a role, such as attempts to make cooperation bilateral, to export finished products in order to achieve a better foreign trade position, and so on.

The movement toward international production specialization and cooperation is not strong enough and thus not efficient enough. Present agreements are restricted to the existing national economic structures, and they do not take into account possible future changes. Measures promising immediate returns predominate over the coordinated development of specialization and cooperation.

7. State and Enterprise Interests in Specialization

The basic purpose of international specialization is to raise the efficiency of national production. Specialization may thus be advantageous for a country even if the productive enterprise directly affected does not immediately earn higher profits. By reducing the range of engineering or other products to be developed or produced, the country gets the chance to concentrate its intellectual and material resources and to increase the efficiency of their use.

Profitable development of international production specialization is in the interest of every CMEA country. Thus a given country is interested in the whole process of such specialization. On the one hand, it must give up established or projected lines of production and meet its needs for a given product from other member countries. On the other hand, it must increase production and exports of the products in which it specializes in order to satisfy the needs of the other countries.

Theoretically we assume that the interests of the enterprise are identical with those of the national economy. But practice proves this is not always the case. Let us consider the following:

  a. The interest of the enterprise is fundamentally influenced

Specialization and Cooperation Projects

if, through agreement on product specialization between countries, it obtains new markets for its products, and if it can avoid the independent development of some new product or save the cost of buying a license. On the other hand, some of its products may be eliminated or changed. Therefore, if the enterprise could continue to sell its products in traditional markets, its interest in specialization will be very low. It will be even lower if the decision is made to close down existing production lines.

b. The interest of the enterprise is influenced if through specialization it can increase profits by means of greater mechanization, better tools, advantages to be derived from the division of labor, capital savings, etc. This aspect of enterprise interest is also equivocal. With some kinds of production specialization, in fact, the enterprise may not perceive the savings that exist on the national economic level. Specialization among countries may also be implemented in such a way that large-scale production is not achieved for the producing enterprises. For example, a country may commit itself to supplying some types of lathes on the basis of a specialization agreement. If the volume involved is small, it may do so without utilizing large-scale production. The enterprise affected may turn out several other products and may not perceive the advantages of specialization.

c. In the majority of cases production specialization among countries may not mean that the enterprises can decide in common on what to develop from each other's products for the new family of products. The enterprises may not be able to decide whether to coordinate further development and the production of standardized parts. Such specialization does not always entail common production techniques, tools, etc. Thus the enterprise will look at the questions of profitability and efficiency only in terms of improving its own product pattern. And this does not always coincide with improving international economic efficiency.

Enterprises are also reluctant to engage in cooperation because a highly regular and reliable supply of parts and units and their quality are not always assured. Disturbances in the rhythm of deliveries hinder the production of partners participating in the cooperation and may cause major losses as well. The socialist international economic mechanism has not yet made possible direct relations among firms cooperating in production. The producers and users of parts and units make contact through industrial ministries and foreign trade bureaucracies, which can often cause long delays. Therefore cooperation in parts, units, and technology relying on the interests of the enterprises requires direct relationships among the firms.

Cooperation among enterprises is also slowed by the fact that the spare parts supply for imported machinery and equipment is not adequate; in some countries even domestic parts supply is inadequate.

While in the case of specialization in finished products among countries, the producing enterprises depend primarily on the domestic supply system for materials and supplies, in the case of international cooperation there is great dependence on foreign supplies. This requires great discipline in deliveries; otherwise cooperation loses its sense and deprives the cooperating firms of potential economic gains.

On the other hand, enterprises have an interest in cooperation because development costs are lower — much lower than they would be if products had to be developed independently. Furthermore product development is accelerated. This leads to a better market position. As a result of cooperation enterprises can achieve production in large series with better tools and lower costs. Enterprises achieve greater mechanization, more precise workmanship, and improved quality. Modern technologies are adopted much more quickly, and investments are paid off more quickly.

Enterprises can also obtain additional savings by joint deliveries to third markets. The costs of market research, market organization, and advertising can be reduced through coordinated marketing. These costs can be reduced even further if the parties create a joint company for sales. Parts supply, service, making repairs under guarantees, and so on, can be-

Specialization and Cooperation Projects

come easier and can enhance the trust of buyers in the cooperating enterprises.

Conflicts of interest between the state and the enterprise may hinder cooperation. Interest in enterprise profit does not always accord with such problems as the balance of payments with the country in question. For example, a surplus in the balance of payments may not seem desirable, even if it comes in the form of surplus deliveries of machinery.

There may be a contradiction between enterprise and state interests when the state wants to expand the production of certain products while curtailing that of others. Or the state may find it undesirable to further strengthen the monopolistic position of some enterprise on an advanced technological level. In such a case the development of competition requires creating another domestic enterprise or changing production lines. However, cooperative relationships among countries require joint activities precisely with enterprises with higher technological standards. As can be seen, this may conflict with the interests of the state.

8. Problems of Large-Scale Specialization Agreements

Large-scale specialization projects, such as the olefin chemistry project with the Soviet Union, the motor vehicles program, and the computer program, are motivated by two factors. One is the interest of member countries in expanding their capacity to produce intermediate products at optimal scales. Surplus production is then exported to other CMEA or third countries. The second motivation is modernization of process technologies and product development. In the first case large-volume production is necessary; in the second, modernization must take place in conjunction with similar developments in other member countries. Specialization programs can also serve as tools for implementing certain domestic industrial development programs.

However, these programs must not lead to the isolation of the CMEA market from the world market. In fact, it is precisely through these agreements that East-West cooperation can become successful. The CMEA market, with its huge potential, provides an opportunity to boost production to attain large, optimal scales of production. Once they are achieved, production for third-market exports can begin. These exports have two objectives: to earn the necessary hard currency for machinery imports needed for development, and to constantly expose the products produced in the framework of CMEA cooperation to the quality requirements and judgment of the world market.

These major specialization projects are decided on by the national governments. The government concludes the obligatory annual or longer-term agreements on the exchange of commodities. Efficiency and profitability are — as in every cooperative venture — highly important, but they do not play active roles in every phase of decision-making. This stems from the extensive model of production integration, from the need to balance exports and imports bilaterally, and from the physical targets set at the outset. The secondary role of profitability can be seen in the fact that at the time of decision-making, usually neither the export-import prices nor the costs of exports are known. But this is generally no obstacle to concluding the related interstate agreements. The agreements generally leave prices open; yet prices ultimately determine the efficiency of the project, and thus the problem usually emerges during the implementation phase.

There is a similar problem with enterprise interests in these agreements. When the interstate frameworks are established, enterprise interests do not play significant roles. In the preparatory stage of these projects, enterprise interests may assert themselves if these projects were initiated by the enterprises themselves. However, the investments necessary for the implementation of agreements are usually provided in the form of state investment or from central development funds.

The bulk of the new major cooperation projects are a serious burden on the balance of payments in convertible currencies. This burden may occur on a single occasion if the initial ma-

Specialization and Cooperation Projects

chinery is imported, or it may be continuous if imports are necessary for ongoing production. Another aspect of the problem is that production integration agreements on specialization and cooperation are successful only if they make it possible to develop exports salable on any market. Otherwise the burden on the balance of payments in convertible currencies will become unbearable, and this will affect CMEA production integration itself. In these proposals, therefore, we must not pursue CMEA autarky; rather we should evaluate the proposals from the standpoint of East-West cooperation and, in general, of linking the CMEA to the world economy.

9. Conclusions

1. Mass and large-series production are only one, and not necessarily the decisive, motivation for the development of specialization and cooperation within the CMEA. This means that the problems of specialization and cooperation from the point of view of concentration of production are not the most pressing, and there are many indications that focusing on these problems tends to mislead us in the pursuit of economic integration. The basic problem is the predominance of finished products, inadequate development of specialization in the production of parts and components, and thus a reduction in the effect of economic forces on further development of CMEA production integration.

2. Individual countries must solve their own internal cooperation problems in accordance with their economic mechanisms and political and social conditions. This by no means applies only to the small CMEA countries. In view of the fact that the Soviet engineering industry is of decisive importance within the CMEA, as regards its role both as a buyer and as a supplier, major attention should be concentrated on promoting internal cooperation in the Soviet engineering industry and in Soviet industrial production, ending autarky, and analyzing opportunities for technological cooperation. At the same time, in each CMEA

The Future of Socialist Economic Integration

country, enterprises must be guided by economic forces toward economic rationality in cooperation and specialization. This means a shift from extensive to intensive methods of integration.

3. In the literature on this subject authors generally emphasize specialization in finished products. This type of specialization is limited by trade and monetary relations and by the extensive production integration model. International price policy, the rigidity of quotas, the need for bilaterally balanced trade, the lack of direct enterprise incentives, difficulties with compensation, and to no small extent, the fact that the use of the instruments of state control encounters conflicting national interests also limit the growth of specialization. Therefore, under the present extensive model for CMEA production integration, cooperation can only be successful if it is based on maximum consideration of the potential of the national economies for internal development.

4. When the national economy specializes in a sector, decisions on the macroeconomic level must be made so that parts production and components production can be planned around the production of finished products. Hungarian motor vehicle production has been a successful case of production integration precisely because it has centered around products that could be sold on a number of markets (buses, rear axles, special trucks) and for which the integrated production of components could be developed.

5. Attention should be directed to the structure of enterprises in the national economies, with particular regard to industry, in the search for futher opportunities for CMEA production integration. Research must determine: favorable conditions for technological progress, the desirable degree of industrial concentration, possibilities of attaining optimal plant size, the formation and maintenance of vertical relations, convertibility of industrial capacity, minimization of inventories, manpower mobility, and possibilities for regional development. We must also bear in mind that although in principle socialist systems of economic management are identical, a number of special na-

Specialization and Cooperation Projects

tional features exist in each CMEA country. For example, in Hungary markets are of greater importance, and the economy is more open. Thus we must also study questions of enterprise autonomy, interindustrial relations, optimal plant and enterprise size, enterprise structure, horizontal relations, monopoly versus competition, and enterprise management.

6. Member countries are moving away from the stage of extensive development. A new stage in socialist industrialization may follow if we take into consideration the requirements of the new, intensive stage. National economies have performed well in the extensive stage, but the pace of international economic change is increasing in the transitional stage. Unfortunately, two characteristics of the previous stage remain:

a. specialization among countries continues to be in finished products. Member countries continue to fail to coordinate research and development efforts and to neglect specialization in components and subassemblies;

b. research continues to be disassociated from production. Here too we need a breakthrough in unifying market and production integration.

Chapter III
Scientific and Technical Cooperation in Production Integration

1. The Importance of Cooperation

Effective economic development in the CMEA countries calls for the acceleration of scientific and technical progress. In this context technical and scientific cooperation among the member countries of the Council for Mutual Economic Assistance is of ever greater importance. Limitations on resources for research, especially in the smaller CMEA countries, require cooperation and an international division of scientific research work. Cooperation makes it possible to carry out scientific research and planning work with less effort and expense over a shorter period.

However, scientific and technical cooperation is not only important for the small countries. The research and production facilities of the CMEA countries make possible the development of the scientific and technical potential of the Soviet Union as well and would lead to the creation of a vast international scientific research and development complex. According to calculations by the Soviet economist O. T. Bogomolov, specialization and cooperation in the CMEA in the area of science and technology would mean savings of around 9 to 11 billion rubles for the Soviet Union in scientific and technical development expenditures in 1980, and about twice this sum for other CMEA countries.[1]

Scientific-Technical Cooperation

The CMEA countries have a vast potential for scientific and technical cooperation. According to GDR sources, world trade in licenses and know-how in the midseventies was distributed as follows:[2]

among the advanced capitalist countries, 63%;
between the advanced capitalist and the developing countries, 3%;
East-West license flow, 10%;
among the socialist countries, 24%.

The capitalist countries thus handle around two thirds of the world trade in licenses. The proportion of East-West license trade is still relatively low but has the most rapid growth rate. The circulation of licenses and scientific and technical documentation among the socialist countries also represents a substantial part of total world trade.

The CMEA countries are net license importers. Their total earnings from license exports in the mid-1970s were estimated at $30 million, which represents only 1% of total world license trade turnover. In the unofficial opinion of Polish experts, for example, the value of Polish license purchases is at least ten times that of sales.

These proportions are also extremely low in view of the fact that 33% of the world's scientific researchers work in the CMEA countries and annually submit 40% of all world patent applications.[3] In short, although the CMEA represents a large proportion of world scientific potential, the exchange of licenses and inventions in CMEA trade is still not sufficiently developed. This also leads us to the conclusion that extensive methods of cooperation must be increasingly replaced by economic methods in the growth of integration in research and development.

2. Payments Related to Cooperation in Research and Development

Until recently payments related to scientific and technological cooperation between the member countries were regulated by the resolution of the Second Session of the CMEA in Sofia.

The Future of Socialist Economic Integration

Licenses and documentation were handed over free of charge; only the actual costs of preparing the documentation had to be paid. This amounted in practice to actual printing costs; the parties did not charge each other for the value of the technical and intellectual knowledge.

For a long time the "Sofia principle" promoted the development of scientific and technological relations, especially through help provided by the Soviet Union to the other member countries. In the course of cooperation over a quarter of a century, the USSR supplied the other socialist countries with about 76,000 technical descriptions and product and material samples in exchange for about 18,000 similar documents.

But the experiences of recent years have shown that a rigid application of the Sofia principle retarded development and cooperation and, through them, technical progress. Since the end of the sixties it has increasingly been pointed out that payments should be made not only for the printing costs of the documents but also for the costs incurred in the course of scientific research and technological development. This would make the countries, enterprises, and institutions involved more interested in developing scientific and technological cooperation.

One retarding effect of the principle of the free exchange of intellectual products is that export-oriented industries are loath to share their knowledge because of potential competition.

Conflicts with foreign trade interests have occurred most frequently in the fields of telecommunications, precision engineering, pharmaceuticals, and medical instrumentation. Only the USSR has had no conflicts of foreign trade interests with the other socialist countries. This has led to an exchange of technological know-how in which bilateral Soviet relations have been strongly preferred.

The Sofia principle was also troublesome because it was not properly coordinated with the main directions in international specialization and cooperation in production. Difficulties also emerged in financing joint research and development: costs in the individual countries frequently differ considerably. Finally, as market and monetary relations and profit and financial incentives became more important, it became more and more difficult to conduct scientific and technological cooperation without some method of independent accounting.

Related to these problems is the fact that the national interests of the various socialist countries are influenced by their level of economic development and the form of scientific and technological cooperation they deem most advantageous for themselves. We can see that the more highly developed socialist countries try to apply new, efficient forms of scientific and economic cooperation that use independent accounting and financial incentives. Less developed countries, however, prefer cooperation in which scientific and technological information is provided without charge.

Discussions about this problem continue in the CMEA. The principle and practice of payment for technological transfers have gradually gained ground. Thus, e.g., in Soviet-Hungarian relations a subcommittee on technological-scientific cooperation worked out in 1968 a set of conditions for the further development of technological and scientific cooperation between the two countries. This makes provisions, among other things, for the creation of joint production laboratories and bilateral research and planning collectives, with joint technical-scientific councils. It further provides an opportunity for the partners to exchange technological documentation at appropriate prices, thus enhancing material interests in technological transfers through this contractual system. Similar agreements have been reached with the GDR, Poland, and Czechoslovakia.

Of course, the two forms, i.e., free and paid exchanges, will exist side by side for some time to come. This is related to the fact that the abolition of free exchange requires great circumspection. It would not be desirable, for instance, for some industrially less developed countries of the CMEA community to bear exaggerated financial burdens. On the other hand, the retarding effect of the lack of payments on such relations has to be taken into account.

The Future of Socialist Economic Integration

3. The Relationship between the Purchase of Western Licenses and CMEA Production Integration

Coordination of research activities and purchases of licenses in the CMEA has not yet been sufficiently linked to the coordination of national economic plans. This limits the effect of technological cooperation on production and on cooperation in production. A very important manifestation of this is the coordination of the purchase of Western licenses and their use in production cooperation policy.

Many licenses are concentrated in the motor vehicle industry. Every CMEA country has bought licenses from Western countries related to the production of automobiles or parts. But the purchase of these licenses has not been coordinated: different countries buy different licenses. This has an important impact on the efficiency of production, the bargaining position of the negotiating partners, and the procurement of the latest technology and techniques. The CMEA countries do not utilize the advantages they have from their large production units. The following examples demonstrate this situation.

Bulgaria bought a license for Setra buses from the West German firm Kass Bohrer. Poland produces passenger cars in cooperation with Fiat and PR 110 buses under license from the French firm Berliet. For engines and transmissions, among other things, licenses from British Leyland, the Italian Ducati, the Danish Burmeister and Wain, and the Swiss Sulzer firms are used. Brake parts are produced under license from the West German Bosch GmbH, and starters under license from Textar GmbH.

Romania signed a contract with the French firm Renault under which Dacia 1300 cars are manufactured. Trucks are produced under a MAN license; helicopter parts come under a French SNIAS license.

Hungary uses an MAN lincense in the manufacture of buses.

As is known, the USSR started the production of Zhiguli cars under a license from Fiat. A large number of Western licenses were bought for the Kama Truck Factory.

Scientific-Technical Cooperation

In short, the socialist countries do not have a coordinated license policy with respect to the production of vehicles. Obviously this affects the processes of product specialization and cooperation and demonstrates the need for integration based on market forces and enterprise-level interaction.

4. Recommendation for the Further Development of Scientific and Technical Cooperation

The further successful development of international scientific and technical cooperation among the CMEA countries calls for the following:

1. Coordination of scientific and technical research; planning and design organs must be improved.
2. The principles of socialist international division of labor must be applied more rapidly to joint scientific and technical research.
3. The duplication of scientific research and of planning and design must be eliminated.
4. Opportunities for direct contacts among scientific research institutes and design and planning offices must be increased. The free employment of scientific researchers and practical experts must be made possible among the CMEA countries.
5. The creation of joint scientific research institutes and planning and design offices should be accelerated. In this context a system of financing joint scientific, planning, and design work should be developed. Evaluation by experts from other countries, using economic criteria, of the work carried out by researchers, planners, and designers in different countries should be developed.
6. Provision should be made for the latest scientific and technical results to spread as quickly as possible through the CMEA countries. The exchange of information and joint marketing should be carried out using economic methods.
7. There is an urgent need for the CMEA countries to formu-

late a coordinated patent and license policy among themselves and toward the West.

8. Finally, the most important point in the area of scientific and technical cooperation is that economic methods should be used to encourage international cooperation. The basic condition for effective multilateral international scientific and technical cooperation is a sound, long-term science policy in each socialist country, adequately coordinated on the CMEA level.

This means that the individual socialist countries must "put their own houses in order" by ending the diffusion of national research and development projects and institutes, eliminating duplication, and attaining a level of organization that enables the different national research and development institutes to be effectively linked in international cooperation.

Chapter IV
The Role of International Economic Organizations and Joint Ventures in Production Integration

1. <u>Historical Antecedents of Joint Ventures</u>

After World War II, with the emergence of the Eastern European people's republics, joint enterprises were formed in these countries with Soviet participation. Thus, e.g., in Hungary there were Maszovlet (civil airlines), Maszolaj (extraction and processing of crude oil), and Maszobal (production of alumina and aluminum). The joint enterprises played a very important role in reconstructing the economies of the people's democracies, which had suffered heavy war damage. With their help plants and machinery were rebuilt and economic activities resumed, all on a technological level corresponding to the standards of those times. These enterprises continued to operate in this form until 1952-54 in Hungary, and in some countries even later, e.g., in Romania until 1956-57.

The joint enterprises operated in the form of joint stock companies. All the usual problems of such ventures occurred, that is, transfer of dividends, reinvestment, joint management, fitting into national plans, domestic taxation, and so on. Their dissolution came about as a result of political, rather than economic, factors. This is why the planning and legal, financial, and related problems of operating these enterprises under socialist conditions have not been developed theoretically.

The Future of Socialist Economic Integration

Trade was the primary activity of the CMEA after its creation. In the early fifties joint ventures did not exist. Credits were granted in the CMEA mainly in the form of machinery, equipment, and materials necessary for specific projects and in the form of crediting clearing accounts. When investments were made to increase the production of raw materials, the party granting credit usually claimed a part of the additional production resulting from the investment.

2. The First Stage in the Development of International Economic Organizations

By the early sixties it had become obvious that it was expedient for the CMEA countries to create joint productive, coordinating, and economic organizations. At the June 1962 session of the CMEA, a number of relevant measures were adopted. The resolutions called for the creation of joint research, design, and construction bureaus, interenterprise agreements in certain industrial sectors, and joint ventures in certain high technology sectors.

Other ideas were also proposed. The majority of these proposals are relevant even today. They include:

— an international agency to coordinate the development and production of equipment for the production of semiconductors;

— joint organizations for the development, production, and utilization of ball and roller bearings;

— organization to coordinate the development and production of diesel and electric engines;

— cooperative organization for the production of hydraulic parts;

— international design and construction offices to develop a uniform and universal system for the automatic control of production processes, and so on.

Most of the proposals were for more organized forms of scientific and technological cooperation, but in some cases they also provided for joint organizations in production, distribution, and sales (on third markets).

The more detailed proposals and draft documents rather accurately reflect the limitations of the fully centralized systems of planning and economic control of the CMEA member countries.

According to the ideas then raised:

— The joint organizations would be controlled by higher organs through boards of directors consisting of experts or delegates from the countries. The agreements on founding the organizations would be signed on the level of the Executive Committee of the CMEA.

— The organizations would perform their activities partly in their own frameworks, and in part they would be in direct contact with the development institutes or productive enterprises of the countries, which would get commissions from the joint organizations for some tasks. The economic framework and conditions of the commissions were not regulated in the drafts of the basic documents.

— The organizations would work on the basis of annual work schedules to be approved by the standing commissions on the basis of proposals by the boards of directors.

— The organizations would work out recommendations for the solution of certain problems, to be approved in the same way through the mediation of the board of directors, by the standing committees, or by other higher organs.

— The maintenance costs of the organizations would be covered from the budget of the CMEA Secretariat.

— The fixed assets of the organizations would be secured by the interested countries according to quotas determined in various ways.

— The results of organizations engaged in research and development would be available to the participating countries after decisions on their use by the standing committees.

It can be seen from these ideas that in those times there was an assumption of completely centralized control. There would not have been direct contacts between the joint organizations and the economic organizations and enterprises of the partici-

The Future of Socialist Economic Integration

pating countries, frequently not even in those cases when the joint organization was to be built into the enterprise itself. They did not take into account the highly important problem of economic incentives and left several economic problems unanswered or tried to solve them unrealistically.

One of the most characteristic features of the integration process at that time was that central attention was focused on working out the draft rules of the joint enterprise. In this context a series of seemingly insoluble problems was debated without having any experience to draw on (interstate settlements, price formation for the products of the joint enterprise, covering costs arising in convertible currencies, covering and conversion of operating costs, conversion and distribution of profits, taxation, tariff laws, liquidation procedures, etc.).

In this first round the rules and institutions were not formed gradually; instead, efforts were concentrated on working out the economic, commercial, planning, and legal rules that caused the most difficult problems.

As these high-level decisions began to take concrete shape, proposals for the creation of joint international organizations became ever scarcer. Participating countries lost interest; in some cases countries expressly objected to the organization of various bodies for technical-scientific cooperation or production relations.

By 1968 a total of eleven coordinating and four economic organizations had been founded with Hungarian participation. Of the former, four are in production, three in distribution, two in services; of the latter, two are engaged in technological development, one in production, and one in the financial field.

3. Lessons from the First Stage of Developing Joint Institutions

The general experiences of international organizations set up in the first stage can be summed up as follows:
— The functions of the organizations were defined too broadly

Economic Organizations and Joint Ventures

due to the lack of a precise definition of what was to be done and the lack of a timetable for the gradual implementation of the program.

— The nature of the organizations was never clarified. This was related to the fact that since ministries also perform economic functions, economic units were to carry out official instructions. That is, the agreements on existing organizations were made between ministries, but the obligations had to be met by enterprises that had no say in setting them.

— The scope of authority of the existing joint institutions was narrow; in general they could only make proposals, and with a few exceptions, they could not make decisions. Thus they were unable to enforce implementation of their resolutions in either specialization, foreign trade, or any other field. To this was added the stipulation that strict unanimity was required even for making a proposal. Also, sanctions were unknown. In managing a company the parity principle prevailed (the director and his deputies managed together), which made the operation of these organizations cumbersome.

— Satisfactory coordination of regulations relating to cooperation was missing in every country, and even the earlier commercial laws were not coordinated. Therefore there was confusion in the organizational solutions and procedural rules devised.

— Fitting the joint enterprises into the system of planned economies also caused problems. According to established practice the economic organization is linked to the administrative and economic system of the country in which it is located. But the problem has remained. Parts of the economic systems did not acknowledge the right of the enterprises to independent planning, and the joint enterprises had no patron organ within the countries. (This held both for the coordinating organizations and for joint enterprises.)

— Joint enterprises operating in two or more countries (as does, e.g., Intransmash) are a continuing source of problems. Difficulties are caused mainly by differences in economic systems. Central agencies cannot influence the part of the enterprise operating in their country to the same extent, or foreign trading activity cannot be carried out under the same conditions, or the wage level is different in the countries concerned, meaning that an identical wage level might cause either tension or labor shortages. The reconciliation of such problems with the legal systems of every interested country requires individual, special solutions.

The joint organizations created were set up mainly on the level of state administration, and the outlays entailed in their maintenance are covered even today mostly from state budgets. The boards of directors consist of representatives of government control agencies. Under such conditions the enforcement of decisions by the board of directors depends heavily on the economic systems prevailing in the countries, on the actual interest of the countries and their enterprises, and on the extent to which decisions by the board of directors accord with the plan instructions and other rules affecting the enterprises of the participating countries. For example, the Cooperative Organization for Ball and Roller Bearings worked out the expected development of demand for bearings over several years, but the plans of the participating countries do not ensure that this demand will eventuate. The same organization proposed setting up production of various machine tools making bearings, but this was not followed up by measures to develop production. The organization believed that more direct contacts were necessary in technological and scientific cooperation, but preconditions for them were lacking in several countries. Solving such problems far exceeds the rights of the members of the board, and they cannot enforce their proposals with the competent authorities.

Interstate settlements related to the joint enterprises generally caused a great many difficulties. This is a consequence of the fact that the currencies of the socialist countries are not convertible, and the costs arising in various currencies have to be converted to transferable rubles. The substance of the problem is that these conversions cannot be done in a satisfactory way that is economically well founded.

Economic Organizations and Joint Ventures

In short, the institutions set up were rudimentary with respect to organization and economic function. The organizations and joint enterprises created were expected to rationalize the sectors of specialization and cooperation across national boundaries. Since production integration can be applied only within very narrow macroeconomic limits, and even less in the microsphere, the proposals and ideas inevitably became unrealistic.

4. Discussions and Preparation for Subsequent Stages of Development and Their Results

After 1968 and prior to the elaboration of the Comprehensive Program, a broad circle of theoretical and applied Hungarian economists discussed the experiences of the joint institutions. Among their conclusions, in my opinion, the following were significant:

1. The potential of socialist international integration had not been utilized prior to 1968.

2. The development of joint organizations and enterprises should not be conducted as a campaign. Interests of the individual countries should be taken into account to set up adequate joint enterprises and interstate organs for precisely delimited tasks.

3. The formation and expansion of joint enterprises should proceed gradually. Initially, emphasis should be placed on the formation of loose coordinating organizations, and the main task should be defined in the organization of certain economic activities (research, prices, markets, salable quantities) and certain functions (mutual sharing of information, standards, etc.). Then the joint organizations should gradually embrace an ever widening sphere of economic activities.

4. Joint enterprises should display a great variety of organizational forms. It is important that the main objective not be form but adaptation to the economic tasks. First, the purpose of the economic cooperation should be defined, and the form of the joint enterprise or organization should be shaped accord-

ingly. The process might start at cooperation in the form of a loose economic association or union, later to be replaced by a tighter form in which the enterprises, while retaining their independence, delegate some functions to the joint interenterprise organizations. Such an organization could be transformed in the course of further development into a united enterprise.

5. The process outlined should also go on in the realm of decision-making and voting procedures. Initially, decisions can be made within the organization in the form of recommendations. Later, however, binding resolutions can be passed. Similarly there may be an evolution in the mode of making decisions. Unanimous decisions could be replaced by a qualified or simple majority. Uniformity is not necessary throughout the whole CMEA. In some areas or in the relations between certain countries there is from the outset an opportunity to use more advanced methods and forms; in other areas or for other countries, however, looser forms of organization may persist.

6. As for the legal form of the joint enterprises and organizations, in view of the experiences up to that point, joint stock companies seem most expedient. They best assure flexible handling of the problems related to the influence of governments and those of ownership. The joint stock company form also is best suited to bridging differences between the various economic mechanisms. By using this form the state can stay in the legal background or come to the fore as it wishes, since it is only indirectly responsible for the operation of the company.

7. The connection of the joint institutions with national planning can cause problems because the economic systems differ to some extent. As regards Hungary, we see no particular problems in the new system of economywide planning. Considering, however, the planning systems of other member countries, the following principles require discussion:

a. In the framework of national planning, the greatest possible degree of independence of the joint institutions must be provided in day-to-day management and, to a certain extent, in investment.

b. Considering the potential of national planning, the right to independent foreign trade should be granted to the joint enterprises.

c. Because of prices, preferences, and other problems, the joint enterprise should be handled as a foreign company in the country affected.

d. The need for direct contacts between enterprises means that national planning should consider shipments within the joint enterprises as those within a factory.

8. Problems of financial settlements related to the operation of joint enterprises require separate discussion. The lack of convertibility and of set rates of exchange of national currencies causes problems in joint enterprises when shipments between the enterprises of the various countries, investments, renewals, production costs and profits, or foreign exchange rates have to be determined. Clarification of these problems is closely related to securing the financial interest of the enterprises.

9. The international involvement of enterprises should not be confined to participation in joint enterprises alone. Besides creating joint enterprises, companies of other CMEA countries could operate affiliates in Hungary. Their administrative centers, factories, and marketing organizations would be in the "parent" country, and major decisions would be made there. The affiliates would be responsible to the center for local sales and potential production problems in Hungary. Their staff and administration could come from the enterprise of the parent country, but they might employ Hungarian labor as well.

The creation of such affiliates seems necessary for customer service, commercial representatives, sales networks, parts warehouses, etc. The Hungarian economic mechanism today provides the basic legal and economic conditions for the operation of affiliates of other CMEA countries.

10. The promotion of direct relations among national enterprises is of fundamental importance.

The Future of Socialist Economic Integration

5. The Second Stage of Development of International Economic Organizations

The second stage in the development of international economic organizations and joint enterprises following the elaboration of the Comprehensive Program began in the early seventies. In this stage some international economic organizations were formed on the basis of CMEA recommendations, and in general, all member countries participate in them. These institutions operate independently, but at regular intervals they report to the competent CMEA organizations. There are also organizations that were set up by certain member countries and in whose activities only interested member countries participate. But the latter organizations also operate according to the basic principles of CMEA cooperation. On January 1, 1980, Hungary was participating in forty-four joint CMEA institutions.

In connection with the creation of these organizations in the last two or three years, a number of problems had to be solved, including planning problems, specific aspects of the introduction of independent accounting, pricing problems, financial relations, credit, material and technical supply issues, and some legal questions.

In 1975-76 the organizations were basically in a start-up state and achieved only preliminary results. However, the initial momentum of the program has been followed by stagnation.

Why is it that things have come to a halt after the initial upswing? Why have well-founded doubts arisen regarding the further development of international economic organizations and joint enterprises?

It is commonly thought that the joint enterprises and international organizations are multilateral in nature in the CMEA, when in fact the principles and practices of bilateralism have predominated both in foreign trade and financial relations, as well as in specialization in manufacturing.

The contradiction between directive national planning systems and the creation of joint enterprises has been recognized. That is, the issue of what the relation should be between the

Economic Organizations and Joint Ventures

joint enterprises and organizations and the national planning agencies has not yet been resolved. According to some people the joint enterprises and international organizations should be subordinate to the central planning organ of the country in which they are located, and their activities should be fitted into the system of obligatory national plan indicators and norms established by the central planning agency. According to others, however, taking this road would conflict with the basic principles of the CMEA. The logic that requires joint enterprises and international organizations to be set up also demands world standards in productivity and technology. If we neglect this principle and follow the road of national standards, it makes no sense to reallocate investment into less developed areas or to countries that apply planning, material consumption, and productivity norms that fall below world standards.

It is worth noting that the existing international organizations have complained that they have received neither data from the participating countries when making their plans nor means and money for the transition to independent accounting systems. The disharmony between the international financial organizations and the activities of joint enterprises and international organizations is obvious. For example, the International Investment Bank may grant credit, in principle, only to profitable organizations, but it should be quite clear that such a position does not take into account temporary start-up losses. It should be equally obvious that planning issues, the system of plan indicators, financial settlements, and legal problems also lack coordination, while the need for an overall coordinating organization is growing.

It is also quite clear that there are conflicts between the international economic organizations and the work of the standing sectoral commissions of the CMEA.

I therefore conclude that the conditions for the massive organization of joint organizations and joint enterprises have not yet emerged in terms of prices, financial arrangements, the conditions of independent accounting, and planning.

From the Hungarian point of view the development of organizations has again turned into a campaign to form new organizations. The point is that there is a conflict between the development of joint organizations as part of the process of extending integration and the fact that the interests of the individual countries in the operation of the organizations and in the precisely defined tasks of the particular industries have not been thoroughly explored.

As a matter of fact, even the problem of gradualness has not yet been unequivocally clarified. In principle everyone agrees that a gradual approach is essential in setting up joint organizations, yet the varying interpretations of gradualness in different countries cause problems. In my opinion a gradual approach should be applied first by stressing the formation of loose coordinating organizations. Their main tasks would be certain economic activities (research, pricing, marketing, exchange of parts, etc.) and functions (mutual exchange of information, standards, etc.). Once the activity has started, emphasis can be shifted to tasks closer to day-to-day management.

The point is that joint enterprises must be started on the basis of the unity of production and market processes; one cannot begin here with production integration. It seems that we have somehow started from the wrong end. In order to promote specialization and cooperation and to solve existing problems in production, we have tried to develop joint enterprises within the existing institutional framework of the CMEA.

6. Sovereignty and Joint Ventures

The argument above suggests that in our era truly efficient forms of international economic cooperation that promote development necessarily enhance elements of mutual interest and mutual dependence.

This implies that if a country does not intend to follow an autarkic economic policy, it must restrict itself to some degree.

Socialist states follow a dialectic process of simultaneous expansion of state sovereignty and deepening self-restriction.

Economic Organizations and Joint Ventures

Social ownership of the means of production expands the scope of state sovereignty. But the activity of the socialist state extends beyond controlling the domestic economy to the control and development of international economic integration. In this context the state undertakes an increasing number of international commitments that affect the national economy, and hence it voluntarily restricts its sovereignty.[1]

But these principles are not accepted uniformly by the CMEA countries. Some contend that working out uniform plans for the member countries and the creation of a joint planning agency, interstate production associations covering whole industries, joint enterprises owned by several countries, and the like, seriously infringe on the independence and sovereignty of the member states.

It is not necessary to criticize this position here in detail. I think it is sufficient to state that the sovereignty of the socialist states develops amidst contradictory trends. On the one hand, the sovereignty of these countries is increasingly secure, and on the other hand, the individual socialist countries voluntarily delegate part of their sovereignty to joint forums developing in the course of international cooperation. In the course of this development some small countries become participants in decisions affecting several countries; thus the scope of their sovereignty is expanding as well.

7. The Division of Profits

Another theoretical problem is whether in the course of the operation of joint enterprises an undesirable redistribution of profits might take place. There are those who believe that the net income created by a country's working class belongs only to the working class of that country.

It should be obvious, however, that insofar as joint ventures are operating in that country, the profits created must be distributed. The question is, therefore, whether it is true that the attraction of foreign capital and its operation in a socialist

The Future of Socialist Economic Integration

country lead to an undesirable redistribution of profits.

To answer the question, we must take into account the basic features of the economic development of the socialist countries. The monetary system established in these countries and the relative underdevelopment of trade and monetary relations do not allow international money and capital movements to affect the economy.

The monopoly on currency and foreign trade, as interpreted in the national plans and the corresponding currency system of the socialist countries, dictates that credits are always resorted to first. From the monetary point of view, credit is in fact a simpler solution because the monopoly on currency and foreign trade neutralizes the world market effects of capital flows on the domestic economy.

Thus capital moves among CMEA countries in the form of credit in the overwhelming majority of cases.

Hence if production integration that relies on extensive methods prevails and foreign assets are borrowed, the problem of the distribution of profits created in the individual national economies becomes political.

Some argue simplistically that since interest is paid on the foreign credits, the workers do not obtain the entire income from their labor and an undesirable redistribution of income occurs. But interest is charged on credits because the country granting the credit draws from its own national economy wealth that could be used in production and would provide net income; those assets are now ceded to another country. The debtor country receives through the credit additional means with which it increases its production and earns new income. It hands over a part of the new income created to the creditor country in the form of interest.

This same argument applies to joint enterprises in the socialist countries, where profits are also distributed.

Thus under socialism profits are redistributed both in the case of credit operations and in the case of joint ventures. In the case of credit operations this occurs indirectly, while in joint ventures it is direct. The difference between the levels of interest and the profit to be transferred is justified by the different risks taken by creditors and investors. With international credit operations, the risk of the creditor is minimal, since loans are guaranteed by interstate agreements. The situation is different with the joint enterprises, where the foreign party's return depends on the venture's profitability. In addition, the socialist state may tax the profits prior to their final international distribution.

The difference between the levels of interest and profits is due not only to different levels of risk but also to the rate of interest between the socialist countries being unrealistically low at present. This is influenced by such factors as the relatively low level of capital flows, not always influenced by commercial motivations, the principles of mutual aid, and so on. But this is not due to the operation of joint enterprises, nor is it true that an undesirable redistribution of the net income created by the working class of the given country takes place. Indeed, in the process of international economic cooperation, capital flows must occur. Capital flows between socialist countries may appear in the movements of credit and investments in joint enterprises. In both cases the same economic process takes place.

8. The Role of the Profit Motive in the Creation and Operation of International Economic Organizations

The profit motive has two roles. On the one hand, in the process of integration it will become necessary for CMEA member countries to finance or absorb capital flows to each other. It follows that one of the conditions for the efficient movement of large amounts of capital is development of the international financial mechanism of the CMEA.

On the other hand, a similar development is also needed within the member countries. The possibility of capital flows is closely related to whether the control systems of the economies, as well as the socialist international monetary system,

The Future of Socialist Economic Integration

make these flows possible.

Our question, then, is how joint enterprise profits can be used to spur the creation of joint enterprises. Here we must look at the role played by enterprise profit motivation in creating joint enterprises. This is a difficult task because the role of profit motivation is different in the individual CMEA countries and because the transferable ruble has deficiencies as an international currency. It functions poorly as a measure of value, means of payment, and reserve currency; its direct transferability is extremely restricted; and for the time being, it is not a general equivalent for commodities. These circumstances prevent the free flow of capital necessary for joint ventures and the division and transfer of profits. Lacking a freely convertible currency, capital flows and profits can take place only in commodity form.

Second, enterprises often do not earn profits on the basis of comparative advantage because prices do not consistently reflect real value relations and because exchange rates are unrealistic. To this is added the fact that the measurement of comparative advantage itself entails great uncertainties. This is a serious problem because this fact in itself may lead to countries refraining from joint efforts.

Due to these factors, in this stage of integration capital transfers will be made by the central government and not by enterprises. Enterprises in socialist countries will not reach a legal and economic position that would allow them to initiate foreign ventures on their own. However, the importance for domestic enterprises of creating joint enterprises will increase if prices are more flexible and rates of exchange work more or less uniformly.

The fact that until a higher stage of development has been attained, only capital flows based on state considerations can be expected is important in two respects. On the one hand, the economies of the socialist countries will in the foreseeable future still be characterized by a relative shortage of capital. On the other hand, the minimum criteria for the profitability of investing capital are different on the enterprise level, besides being more easily quantifiable from those calculated on the state economic level.

For these and other reasons, only at a time when socialist integration is stronger can we expect capital movements to joint enterprises in which the main motive will be greater returns on capital relative to domestic conditions. Until then capital flows among the CMEA member countries will be determined on the intergovernmental level.

9. Harmony between National Planning Systems and the Development of Joint Enterprises

Some opinions hold that the central planning agency of the country in which a joint enterprise is located needs full authority over all the planned activity of the enterprise. According to this view the central planning agency of the country where the joint enterprise is located would set the obligatory plan targets and norms for the enterprise according to the requirements of the national economic plan of the country and taking into account the particular features of the given organization.

However, if the joint enterprise is built into the system of obligatory plan indicators of the country in which it is located, then, evidently, the standards used within the country in question will prevail (material and labor inputs, productivity prescriptions, financial indicators relating to efficiency, etc.). Yet the principles and mechanisms regarding returns, efficiency norms, and self-financing differ considerably by country. For example, the methods for measuring inputs and comparing them with output, the determination of production costs, and the use and distribution of income differ greatly by countries. If we add to all this differences between socialist countries in pricing, it is not hard to see that an obligatory application to the joint enterprises of the norms of the country of location does not necessarily ensure greater productivity throughout the CMEA. The problem is that if the productivity standards of the

The Future of Socialist Economic Integration

country of location are lower than those of other CMEA countries, then it is precisely the main rationale for setting up socialist joint enterprises, e.g., greater productivity, that is neglected. Obviously the only way out of this tangle is to apply either average CMEA norms (regarding raw material inputs, labor, productivity, etc.) or the norms of the leading CMEA countries, which would allow an even more rapid increase in efficiency. In the latter case the increase in efficiency is most obvious.

The problem here is that if we follow the course of the most rapid rise in efficiency, then, on account of differences in economic development, the location of the joint enterprise in the less-developed countries would not seem efficient. On the other hand, if we applied the norms of a less-developed country, instead of a rise in efficiency on the CMEA level, there might be a drop because we would be drawing investments and capital from countries on the technological frontier. This suggests that the location of joint enterprises cannot be primarily determined by CMEA-level efficiency or optimum criteria.

Chapter V
New Methods of Production Integration: Target Programs

1. The Need for New Methods

By the midseventies the conditions of economic growth differed considerably from those that had prevailed when the Comprehensive Program was drawn up, i.e., between 1968 and 1971. The CMEA economies had to respond to the problems caused by the new situation in the world economy. Economic growth in the CMEA countries had been quite rapid over the previous twenty-five years and had attained 5.9% per year in the seventies. For continued growth at that rate, stable supplies of raw materials, full use and training of available labor, a high rate of investment and its most efficient use, promotion of the division of labor among the CMEA countries and with the Western countries, a dynamic research and development policy, and the adaptation of planning methods to changing economic requirements are needed. These requirements have made the search for new methods of integration necessary.

Coordinating and integrating plans has been a primary method of socialist integration. However, there are now two central problems which face long-run planning in the CMEA.

One problem is energy and choosing an appropriate energy policy. There is a great need to adapt to higher energy prices in order to overcome the consequences of the raw material and energy crisis and to formulate a new raw material and energy policy. The plans of the individual countries for 1976-80 reflect a selective investment policy that was applied to the development of sources of raw materials and energy. However, it is conceivable that during the 1981-85 plan period, specialization and cooperation will take center stage in the target programs. The Twenty-ninth Session of the CMEA in Budapest and the new plan for integration reflect the huge efforts made by the member countries in joint exploration and exploitation of natural resources in the USSR.

The other main problem is that attempts to raise productivity must be accelerated, especially in those countries where the proportion of workers in agriculture is low, or where the available reserves of labor are rapidly declining.

A new method of planning target programs has been adopted to deal with these problems. These projects represent a new, concrete step in economic cooperation among the member countries and in the planned development of socialist integration.

The most important aspect of these projects is that they are comprehensive. They cover the whole development of the area, from scientific research to the launching of products, from the exploitation of natural resources to the development of processing machines. Naturally they also provide for the most effective forms of the division of labor.

2. Dimensions of the Target Development Programs

The long-term target development programs are designed to help assure supplies of some important materials and products to the CMEA countries.

Planned target programs were presented in the plan for integration adopted at the Twenty-ninth Session of the CMEA.[1] The first section of the plan covers projects to be carried out through the joint efforts of the member countries. Their combined value is about 9 billion transferable rubles, of which 7.5 billion were to be invested between 1976 and 1980. Of the ten

Target Programs

projects planned, eight are to be built in the Soviet Union through joint efforts of the member countries. They are the following:

— exploration of the Orenburg natural gas deposits in the Urals and the construction of a 3,000-km-long pipeline from Orenburg to the Western frontier of the Soviet Union;

— joint construction of a 750kV power transmission line;

— construction of a cellulose plant with an annual 500,000-ton capacity;

— construction of an asbestos combine with an annual 500,000-ton capacity;

— expansion of capacities yielding ferrous ores;

— expansion of ferroalloys capacities;

— creation of a modern fodder-yeast plant;

— creation of a center for training civil airline specialists.

Two other projects to be set up through joint efforts are:

— a nickel- and cobalt-processing plant in Cuba;

— expanding the telecommunication systems of the member countries.

This section of the plan specifies the deliveries and investments the individual countries are to contribute to the completion of the projects. The countries interested in certain development objectives — e.g., in additional supplies of sources of energy, raw materials, and certain agricultural products — supply certain products, specified in physical terms, in advance, on credit. The claim on credit is due to the fact that the supplies are usually used to expand capacity in the country where the source of energy or the raw material is located. To this end, adequate machinery, equipment, steel products, and fittings are needed. One major feature of the agreements is that the energy and raw material exports and the counterdeliveries of materials and machinery are specified in physical units as well as in value.

In mid-1980 the target programs for the five-year plan for 1981-85 were still being formulated. The work was slowed by a host of anticipated and unforeseen economic difficulties.

The Future of Socialist Economic Integration

3. Satisfying Demand through Target Programs

a. Fuels and raw materials, agricultural and food products, consumer goods and transportation are key problems for the member countries in both the medium and the long run. Target programs must be initiated in these areas.

The purpose of the target programs aimed at fuels, raw materials, and electric energy is to investigate what joint efforts would be needed in order to satisfy the long-term demand of the member countries for iron, steel, nonferrous metal products, energy, and chemicals. The main ways to satisfy this demand can include: exploitation of hydroenergy reserves, development of nuclear power stations, development of new sources of energy, and the maximum exploitation of present fuels:

— development of forms of cooperation in whose framework the member countries use their natural resources, labor, and capital to create new extractive and transportation capacities for the product in question. This will be made possible by having the interested countries shoulder the burdens in the same proportion as they share in the new product. Modes of cooperation should be developed that take into account the interests of both exporters and importers. They can be special purpose credits, joint investments, exchange of commodities taking into account capital intensity and other features of production, cooperation in the exploitation of the natural resources of third countries, etc.;

— selection of a rational location for the energy- and raw-material-intensive projects created under cooperation. New energy- and raw-material-intensive processes should be located near the primary energy and raw material deposits, and complete processing should be promoted by simultaneously creating joint extractive and processing enterprises, taking into account the particular features of the locale and the needs of the individual countries. Large extractive and processing facilities in fuels, chemicals, and ferrous and nonferrous metallurgy are of particular merit, e.g., the construction of a high-capacity metallurgical combine in the area of the Kursk iron ore deposits.

Target Programs

Conservation of energy and raw materials should be promoted in every instance; the specific demands of production for energy and materials should be reduced, and to this end, the current achievements of science and technology should be exploited;

— cooperation should be established with third countries for the exploitation of natural resources.

The appropriate scale of demand can be established by determining correct norms for the use of energy, by purposefully modifying the pattern of energy utilization, and by rationally locating energy- and material-intensive processes.

b. In the framework of the target program on agricultural and food products, a plan should be drawn up on a method to satisfy the needs of the member countries for basic agricultural and food products (meat, fish, milk and dairy products, eggs, vegetable oil, sugar, fresh and preserved vegetables and fruits) and for which the sectors' activities must be coordinated to accomplish this. Given the circumstances of the CMEA countries and the importance of agricultural products, a basic guideline is that every member must be in general self-sufficient.

Methods that help solve related tasks are cooperation, by purposefully concentrating investments in: the development and production of machinery and equipment necessary for agriculture, particularly animal husbandry, and for advanced closed production systems; the production of fertilizers and pesticides; the development and application of irrigation equipment; the evaluation of results; the improvement of plant and animal species; solving feed problems; the modernization and development of the food industry; meeting the packaging needs of agriculture and the food industry; the production and modernization of refrigeration equipment, expanding an international chain of refrigeration; setting prices that stimulate the production of scarce commodities; and promoting specialization by using natural endowments.

c. The long-term target development programs of industrial consumer articles also center on products that cause the greatest problems for the member countries, partly with respect to quantity, partly to quality. They include some light industrial products (knitwear, clothing, shoes), furniture, and some household appliances and telecommunication products.

d. The long-term target program of the engineering industry points in two directions. On the one hand, it is called on to assure supplies of machinery and equipment needed for the other target programs; on the other hand, it promotes the modernization, expansion, and structural transformation of the engineering industry itself, which must adapt to solve the first task. Therefore we must establish high-level, rapid, and efficient specialization and cooperation and jointly construct new factories.

4. The Extent of the Target Programs

As can be seen from the draft target programs and the communiqué issued by the Thirtieth Session of the CMEA, a large number of areas could be covered. Around ninety areas are of prime importance. It is mainly on these topics that the countries are attempting to clarify their needs and the possibilities for their satisfaction. However, neither the areas nor the ways in which the individual countries will be involved have been settled.

It can already be seen that the first stage of implementation of specialization and cooperation in manufacturing will not affect the engineering industry. At this stage target programs will only play a role to the extent that they represent the only possible path for obtaining machinery and equipment that cannot be purchased from the capitalist countries, for reasons of foreign exchange, but could be manufactured in our countries. It is improbable that with the attempts to address the much more pressing material supply problems, sufficient energy will remain for independent attention to the idea of target programs in the engineering sectors.

It is also doubtful whether the other main direction of cooperation in manufacturing can be fully pursued, that is, the principle of rational location of production, which, in the case of vital fuels and raw material, calls for the location of primary processing near deposits. However, it is likely that the target programs will cover the new extractive capacities, although machinery and equipment supply will continue in the present way and on the present level.

Even so, the number of areas could be too high for the financial resources and organizational conditions available. It is quite likely that even the new lists to be drawn up in the future will be too long, and important changes will be made in them in the course of implementation.

In spite of all this, the fact that the target programs have been accepted, the depth of their formulation, and the way in which the matter is being handled lead to the conclusion that this action will advance integration, even if at a slower rate than that of our initial, overly optimistic plans.

5. Location of Plants and Satisfying Demand

The formula for the location of plants in the principles of the target programs requires a somewhat detailed analysis.[2] Along with sharing costs and production policies, the problem of efficiency is of great importance. In these terms the rationality of the formula cannot be challenged when the investment costs and the additional costs of primary processing at the site of the deposits are lower for the importing country than the additional cost of transporting the product in an unprocessed state. But this is far from being a necessary, general rule, and circumstances have to be judged in each case individually, through careful analysis. Separate consideration is also needed if the processing plant established at the site of the deposit turns out products of a kind and quality that do not wholly meet the needs of the participating countries. The problems entailed grow if the products cannot be reexported. In short, the formula in question should be considered a rule of thumb rather than a hard and fast law. This has to be particularly emphasized because in the course of preparing the target programs, this principle was rather heavily emphasized, although it can easily lead into a blind alley.

The principle of satisfying demand to a realistic, rational extent is of a different nature and, indeed, has general validity.

Determination of a "realistic, rational extent" can be made for the community only through a collective decision by the countries. The observation of this principle assumes that the member countries see and analyze in depth each other's commodity patterns, their construction and technology situation, and the characteristics of their products, so that they are each capable of judging whether their demands for materials are realistic. They can then also develop for each other proposals to improve the situation. The collective statement of the realistic demand for materials and energy for one's own consumption assumes a detailed knowledge of each other's living standards and consumption policies and the ability to make decisions that are fully acceptable by every country. It should be obvious that such conditions will not come about in the near future for either industrial or personal and public consumption — and until then, attempts to apply this principle would inevitably be piecemeal and coercive.

6. The Principle and the Limitations of Sharing Investment Burdens

The increased raw material production outlined in the target programs demands sharing costs. Planned target programs promise to be similar to those already being implemented, e.g., the cellulose factory at Ust-Ilim, the Orenburg gas pipeline, and so on. These projects make products available to the participating countries in large quantities; on the other hand, at least as regards Hungary, they demand large investments.[3] Theoretically these expensive investments are due to the need to expand capacity; in practice they are also due to the fact that these joint investments are located in areas lacking infrastructure, and the latter must be constructed together with the plants. Furthermore the participating country has little influence on the investment cost calculations made by the country in which the plant is to be located (if only because it will not own the plant nor share the risk of operating it). While the interest on credits granted is set near the socialist market rate [which is quite low], prices on the products shipped to pay for the credits are to be set and revised using the moving average price base.

Hence, although joint investments similar to current ones may help solve some raw material problems in some countries, it is still questionable whether they can become the main solution to the fuel, raw material, and energy problems of the European CMEA countries. Nor can it be seen to what extent these countries can provide the necessary funds for investment.

A different — and no less important — matter is that these actions are favorable for the European member countries politically. Such investments promote a secure supply of raw materials and strengthen the USSR and the member countries economically. The size of the credits granted is obviously limited by the extent of the drain on economic assets from the domestic economies, as seen in terms of domestic policy, the country's material commitments, and its economic objectives. These factors set an ultimate limit. It cannot be doubted, however, that within this limit, it is expedient to make the investment contributions indicated for the reasons just reviewed. The limits arising from the scarcity of domestic resources or investment funds available in the given country fall within this extreme frontier.

These limits were discussed by Tibor Kiss in 1969. He wrote:

> Cooperation in investment is the most backward area in the economic cooperation by CMEA countries. There are several objective reasons for this, as well as many subjective ones.
>
> Development of investment cooperation is badly hindered by the fact that the countries in question are relatively poor in capital (relative to labor), and their economic development levels are different.

The Future of Socialist Economic Integration

In the CMEA countries there are no capital surpluses to be exported; and if capital is still being exported, it must be done at the expense of some other development. This impairs the rate of economic growth. This fact in itself leads to a situation in which every country wants to export capital only in the most necessary cases.

If smaller countries had to secure a large part of their growing imports of fuels and raw materials only with investment contributions, this would inevitably slow down their economic development. In that case employment would cause growing concern, and opportunities to increase the productivity of labor would be very limited.[4]

New aspects of the problem were pointed out by the prime minister of Czechoslovakia, Lubomir Strougal, at the Thirtieth Session of the CMEA:

In our view, the main importance of the long-term target programs is that we prepare long-term solutions for major problems together.... In our opinion it also has to be emphasized that simultaneously with clarifying and working out technological solutions, the volume of the inputs should be compared with the economic potentials of the countries concerned and with the assumed effect of the joint actions.[5]

All this is also desirable because the uncertainties of investment costs for joint projects and of the prices of products to be produced are no less than for other plants. Three are projects in which major increases in investment costs were foreseeable at the start of construction, and the investor tried to shift a proportionate part of the increase onto the participants. Rises in world market prices have a similar effect on the prices of the products set in the agreements. It is self-evident that these two changes both have adverse effects on profitability. Yet such developments can be anticipated in every case in which the interstate agreement underlying cooperation is concluded before a detailed and well-researched cost estimate is available. And this happens rather frequently.

These problems can be easily solved if the investment contributions are handled not as strictly economic but as political issues.

We see a special phenomenon in agriculture and the food industry. It is well known that the CMEA community as a whole has large problems producing adequate amounts of grain, meat, and dairy products. Various target programs reflect this. Yet for the time being, the countries with deficits in agricultural products have not agreed that investment projects to promote agricultural development and the food industry on a community-wide level should be financed under the necessary special terms. The reason is presumably the general scarcity of investment funds and the intention of the countries to use them mainly for industrial development. It seems obvious, however, that the stance of these countries will change as an adequate supply of these commodities becomes an ever more sensitive point of living standards policy. It is thus likely that in the eighties the bulk of free investment funds will be made available for agricultural and food industry development.

7. Coordination of Target Programs and National Planning

The target programs signify great progress in the field of planning cooperation. Some groups of economists hold that the multilateral integration measures and the long-term target programs are forms of cooperation in planning that may later grow into joint planning. However, a series of overly optimistic appraisals of the situation have also appeared. They claim that we should start to jointly select strategic development objectives and to draw up the related international material balances. It has been stated that the plans for integration and the long-term target programs should become organic parts of national economic plans; this means that a start should be made toward transi-

The Future of Socialist Economic Integration

tion from individual national balances to working out joint balances.

If we sum up what has been said about the target programs, we can state that in terms of planning, production integration has reached a new stage. Its substance is that:

— the importance of areas of multilateral cooperation is growing;

— the scope of problems covered by multilateral cooperation is expanding, since the production and technological relations coordinated on a macrolevel between enterprises have been established for longer periods;

— elements of joint planning have emerged.

Some aspects of the target programs with respect to these points will be examined below. However, let us first look at the relationship between target programs and national planning.

Given the present model of planning cooperation, joint planning activity can be expanded within the institutional system of the CMEA only by coordinating national plans.[6]

Thus joint planning must begin with national plans and can be implemented only by taking into account the economic development objectives and sources of investment provided for them. The same holds for major CMEA-wide tasks, such as, e.g., the target programs related to developing sources of raw materials, fuels, and energy and the corresponding creation of plants to produce the necessary machinery, and so forth.

This suggests that the path of development of production integration does not lead through the creation, implementation, and location of target programs determined primarily by the requirements of efficiency or CMEA optima but through the expected success of the program in fulfilling national goals by developing either supplies of raw materials or trade in finished products. Thus, according to the logic of joint planning flowing from the Comprehensive Program, we proceed from the national plan toward the common goal of optimization. It also follows that the resulting optimums and efficiency will be different if we coordinate the national plans, and different again if we reverse the order of planning and compile the national plans by setting out from considerations of community-level optimums and efficiency.

Target Programs

Relying on this premise, several Soviet economists and others from various member countries point out that it seems expedient to reverse the order of planning. By defining pivotal development objectives and strategies, individual countries can plan their own activities in conjunction with clearly formulated joint plans. They can build these projects into their own national plans and economic growth targets and plan for the necessary investment funds.

I think that the system of overall planning proposed promises greater results than does the present one. Yet I feel that if we actually took this road, we would again disregard the present stage of economic cooperation, i.e., instead of unity of production and market integration, we would implement economic cooperation focusing on production integration alone. The institutional agents of this economic cooperation would be the national states, and its basic method would be coordination of the economic development plans formulated in the systems of goals of those states. The basic task is therefore to improve the coordination of national economic plans.

Furthermore the procedure proposed — that is, the implementation of joint planning — does not conform with the present model of cooperation in planning. Rather, it accords with the requirements of the second stage, that of integrated planning, when concepts deriving from the requirements of optimality and efficiency on the community level would determine the allocation of investment. But it is difficult to see it as a guideline for practical activity, since the more developed stage could be the one following the completion of the Comprehensive Program and the improvement of the present forms of plan coordination. Research in this area is, however, still valuable.

Thus, although national planning agencies are unable to choose the most efficient lines of development on the community level, and integrated communitywide planning will eventually be necessary, limited investment funds and domestic constraints now permit only limited supranational planning even through target programs. If, for example, all seventy or so Hungarian industries tried to promote their development by adopting the most efficient methods at the community level, the demand for investments would greatly exceed all the funds available for domestic industrial investment. Because balances have to be drawn up not only for the production of raw materials and for certain priority development projects but also for such goals as personal consumption, the national planning agencies need to make sizable investments in other projects as well. Therefore the differences due to the sizes, objectives, and strivings of international and national organizations must be considered very seriously.

Hence it is very doubtful whether one can agree with the views of N. V. Bautina, the Soviet economist. She writes as follows:

> The socialist countries participate in the mutual exchange of activities to different extents, from which it follows that socialist international specialization is achieved by the different countries to different extents. Those socialist countries which do not show interest in mutual coordination of economic decisions, that is, which do not participate in joint planning activity, do not in fact create conditions for applying what planning has achieved; thus they do not utilize the potentialities inherent in economic cooperation and do not realize important properties of socialism.

I believe a response to this is sufficiently clear from what has been said. It is not as if the national planning agencies were unaware that production decisions implemented within the framework of CMEA-level production integration are more efficient than their own. And it must be acknowledged that national decisions do not take advantage of opportunities inherent in socialist international cooperation. But today we must also cope with the problems that the national states face with regard to their standards of living, the development of their infrastructures, and so on.

8. Some Questions on the Methodology of Planning the Target Programs

The target programs represent a new opportunity for planning. In themselves they impress the observer with their rationality and scale. However, in my opinion we must be careful not to be carried away by the logic of great opportunities and economies of scale lest further disequilibria arise. I mention the following, mainly methodological, questions to show how real this danger is.

a. During the course of the creation and development of joint programs, some countries wanted to be members of as many organizations as possible or to propose as many target programs as possible. The danger of being left out and the knowledge that they will not share in the subsequent benefits or have access to markets acted as strong incentives to participate in as many ventures as possible. However, once they are members, they have trouble coordinating investment requirements and objectives with their available resources and the goals of their national plans, and they become cautious and uncertain in their participation. This leads to the conclusion that a very thorough survey of economic interests and capabilities must be made for both the target programs and for the coordinated planning of integration measures.

b. The planning of target programs is relatively independent of other forms of planning cooperation. In themselves they are supposed to provide a complete link between objectives and resources. But since the target programs cover broad, complex economic problems affecting the CMEA countries as a whole, they significantly affect the economies of each of the different countries. They also call for certain adjustments and modifications in national plans. In this context, therefore, target programs also influence the coordination of five-year plans: to a certain extent they replace them. The big problem is that the coordination of plans for the industrial and foreign trade sectors is not covered by the target programs; this is done through the traditional planning mechanisms. Moreover we are faced with the difficulty that the target programs are operated on the basis of economic efficiency for the CMEA as a whole, while the production of products to pay for them is run on the national level. For example, the joint production of certain raw materials must be paid for in the form of investment goods that we supply as compensation (pharmaceuticals, buses, etc.). But these goods are produced under completely different standards of efficiency and, in many cases, even under different foreign trade prices and financial conditions than the energy and raw materials obtained in exchange for them. Thus planning becomes disjointed and uncoordinated.

c. The suggestion has been made that the number of areas covered by the target programs is now too high. This raises the question whether we are really concentrating attention on the central issues. More precisely, eliminating the backwardness of certain areas of a national economy or eliminating temporary imbalances may, and indeed must, be achieved by concentrating on the decisive "links." The Soviet economist G. M. Sorokin put it very aptly:

> In determining rates and proportions, planning of the national economy constantly encounters a vicious circle of conditions. We must therefore find the point where the circle of conditions can be broken and the decisive link selected from the chain of economic development. To take an example from the history of the Soviet economy: In 1921 a serious situation arose in the Don Basin. All conditions formed a single, uniform circle: there was no wheat because there was no coal, but there was no coal because there was no wheat. What was the way out of this situation? Lenin pointed out that the chain had to be broken somewhere by the workers' energy, willpower, and heroism in order to get the machinery rolling. At the present stage there are other material conditions besides the workers' energy. However, Lenin's thesis for the

methodological approach to the planning of reproduction is still entirely valid.[7]

It is thus perfectly clear that a single problem must be plucked out of the whole set of problems, and it should be the one that will lead to the elimination of all the other problems and of the disproportions in the national economy, thus restoring equilibrium.

Now, if we try to follow the thrust of the present target programs, we can see that we are trying to solve almost all the problems of the CMEA within the framework of the target programs. The feasibility of this approach is contradicted by our experiences to date. It is sufficient in this context to point to the example of the German Democratic Republic's structural policy. Recent planning experiences in the GDR led to the conclusion that rapid simultaneous development of several branches or products without adequate development of the supporting sectors can endanger the implementation of the original program.[8] Thus, approaching all our problems through special purpose target programs requires careful consideration in terms of planning methodology. The fact is that the objectives of the projects have been clarified, but the economic conditions needed for their successful implementation remain vague and have been pushed into the background.

Chapter VI
Regional Development and Production Integration

1. The Problem

Soviet economists were the first to recognize that production integration has affected the regional economic development of the Soviet Union and also that of the smaller CMEA countries. They emphasized that joint development of raw material deposits in the Soviet Union, the creation of joint industrial complexes, the construction of infrastructure, imports of labor from other member countries, and the like have had a great effect on regional development.

In this context regional economics faces the task of forming a theory from the integration experience of the economic regions of the USSR. This task is urgent because of the need of planning and economic agencies to find optimal methods for the participation of the whole economy and its sectors and regions in the international division of labor.

Among the problems of these agencies is optimal location. The optimal location of industry in the USSR is determined, along with several other factors, by the geography of foreign economic relations and integration with the CMEA member countries. In the opinion of Soviet economists, when examining regional problems of the economic integration of socialist countries, it is absolutely necessary to compare and carefully evaluate in economic terms the natural resources of the USSR and the other, smaller member countries. Without an exploration of the physical setting of the socialist international division of labor, it is difficult to work out an efficient model of the division of labor either for the CMEA as a whole or for the USSR and the individual socialist countries.

Regional aspects of socialist economic integration are important for the smaller countries as well. Considering the geographical complexity of the countries participating in production integration, an efficient international system of transportation, including railway lines, high-voltage power grids, pipelines, etc., must be established.

One very important factor in integration over the coming years will be the fact that the Danube will play a growing role as an important north-south transportation artery. In this context the modernization of the north-south lines of the Hungarian railway network also becomes an urgent task. The economic irrationality of rigid national boundaries is perhaps most obvious with regard to various railway lines. We can assume, however, that the broad potential of a transportation-"geographical" union of the European socialist countries has already been recognized.

Some Soviet economists have pointed out that there is great potential for economic integration in the economic regions along the two slopes of the Carpathians, where five socialist countries — the USSR, Poland, Czechoslovakia, Hungary, and Romania — have common frontiers.[1] The authors state that in the area mentioned, there had been no substantial trade before World War II. This was due to the fact that economic relations between the USSR and these countries were at an ebb at the time, and for strategic reasons, industrial plants or main transport lines simply could not be built there.

After 1945 the economic development of these earlier "frozen" areas assumed central importance in the economic relations among the CMEA countries. The fact cannot be neglected that the meeting point of these five countries lies at the center of the industrial map of all socialist Europe. Geograph-

The Future of Socialist Economic Integration

ically it is the closest point to the industrial centers of the European parts of the USSR and those of the European socialist countries. But at present there is relatively little industry in the region itself. In the four countries bordering the USSR, in areas no further than 150 kilometers from the Soviet frontier, industry employed 1.4 million people in 1960 and 2.3 million in 1970 (of the latter, 1.1 million were in Poland, 750,000 in Romania, 300,000 in Hungary, and 150,000 in Czechoslovakia); that represented 21% (in 1960, 17%) of total industrial employment, although the area itself represents 37.4% of the total area of these countries. But in the USSR and the republics bordering on the countries mentioned, that is, in Moldavia, Lithuania, and in eight adjacent regions: Odessa, Chernovtsy, Transcarpathia, Lvov, and Volinsk in the Ukraine, Brest and Grodno in Belorussia, and the Kaliningrad Region in the RSFSR — again including only areas within 150 kilometers of the border — about the same number of industrially employed can be found. In these border areas industrial employment per 100 square kilometers is lowest in the Volinsk, Brest, and Grodno areas and in the Moldavian Republic; they are also the least industrialized (6-8 industrial employees per 100 inhabitants).

While in the Common Market the most important economic region lies in the area of the Rhine, that is, at the meeting point of five countries in the community, and backward areas are usually found on the periphery, the backward areas in the European part of the CMEA lie right at its center. That these areas on the border of the USSR and in the four socialist countries represent an economic vacuum is a heritage from the past.

At the same time, the meeting point of the five socialist countries — that is, the Carpathian region, including the foothills and the adjacent plains — sits at a nodal point in interstate communications. Suffice it to point out that of the five railway lines from the USSR to the European socialist countries, four pass through this area.

In short, the region where the five socialist countries meet has favorable conditions for playing the role of an "industrial bridge" across frontiers. It is true that in this area a high-capacity infrastructure of international importance has emerged, but its further development to a level approaching world standards is needed. This will certainly affect large-scale industry located in the area, primarily ferrous metals and petrochemicals.

2. Some Practical Questions in Regional Planning of the Raw Material and Fuel Base

One of the central ideas of integration and regional development is that the eastern regions of the Soviet Union should increasingly become the sources of raw material and fuel imports for the CMEA member countries. This could be done in such a way that Soviet domestic demand would be satisfied as much as possible from resources near the point of consumption, while the sources for increasing exports would be the eastern regions of the USSR.

The attitudes of the European countries to these ideas are shaped partly by political and partly by economic considerations.

From the political point of view, the European CMEA countries support the idea, for development of the eastern regions in this way strengthens the Soviet economy and thereby increases the international weight of the CMEA community, allowing it to raise its efficiency and expand. On the negative side are the additional investments necessary to develop the eastern regions that could syphon off funds from the domestic economies, possibly causing internal problems.

From the economic point of view, the gradual shift to the east in the sources of additional imports raises this issue: for which products and under what circumstances will these imports remain competitive with other sources of imports in terms of both hard currency costs and economic efficiency? Economic considerations may dictate a lower level of imports than the one established for political reasons. Most likely both considerations will play a role. Thus there will be Siberian projects in which the European member countries will participate for political reasons, and others in which they will participate on economic grounds. However, additional imports of some products will be procured from other sources. For countries with limited capital resources, a third road — that is, imports without "investment contribution" — will be more feasible, even if they are more expensive than imports from the USSR. Moreover, as the costs of these Siberian investments rise, the European CMEA countries in a position to increase the production of some substitute commodities will find it profitable to do so. Increased domestic production can replace some imports, while the member countries that are poor in raw materials will have to compensate by increasing efficiency.

Another consequence for the European CMEA countries is that this considerably widens the geographical area they have to take into account as a source of imports in their cost and efficiency computations.[2] That is, Siberian import prices, burdened as they are with the cost of investments in plant and infrastructure and with high transportation costs, make higher import prices from other areas attractive, even if credits must be granted in order to import.[3]

Thus the profitable import area of the CMEA countries may be considerably expanded.

3. Conclusions

We have found that regional development plays an important role in the economic integration of the CMEA countries. The construction of large, internationally financed industrial complexes and interlocking transportation networks has contributed to the industrial development of the various national regions; at the same time, considerations of regional development have contributed to CMEA integration as a whole.

In the context of regional development we have discussed two problems: the need to develop those border regions which form the center of the European CMEA, and the problems of regional development associated with the exploitation of Siberian sources of energy and raw materials. We maintain that the development of the trans-Carpathian border region has great industrial potential as well as the potential to contribute greatly to strengthening CMEA integration. This area, although industrially underdeveloped, is close to many of the industrial centers of the CMEA and has a good transportation network.

The second problem is that of the development of Siberian sources of raw materials and energy. A process has started whereby the sources of these primary commodities are being shifted to the east. At the same time, an integrated transportation system is being constructed to transport these commodities west. The necessary investments and higher prices for these commodities strongly affect the pattern of CMEA integration.

Chapter VII
Pricing, Market, and Monetary Relations and Production Integration

1. Introduction

Analyses of production integration have clearly shown that the shortcomings of CMEA integration to date are in large part due to the suppression of market and monetary relations. The special commercial policy and market relations existing in international trade within the CMEA in many respects resemble those on the domestic markets of these countries rather than on world markets, which are influenced by international competition.

Market and monetary relations are characterized in production integration by the fact that "the CMEA member countries adopt the basic position that their system of economic and scientific-technical cooperation is based on the general laws of the building of socialism, the basic principles of socialist economic control, and the integral linking of plan coordination as the basic method of cooperation, with the more extensive use of commodity [market] and monetary relations."[1] This passage clearly shows that the basic method of cooperation is plan coordination, and market and monetary relations play a subordinate, secondary role.

International accounts among the CMEA countries are settled

Pricing, Market, and Monetary Relations

in transferable rubles.[2] The payment system corresponds to the present stage of development of integration. This system of accounting ensures, ultimately, the expansion of trade, and it satisfies the needs for short-term credits that arise in the course of bilateral trade. The transferable ruble makes it possible for all CMEA member countries to preserve trade equilibrium over a given period and to make settlements with all other member countries in transferable rubles. However, we make only limited use of the potential of this system to balance accounts multilaterally.

The system is still basically a bilateral one.

The processes connected with modernization of the transferable ruble were largely completed by the midseventies. It is now perfectly clear to us that in the current decade, modernization of the transferable ruble cannot be separated from other forms of economic cooperation. Further development of the transferable ruble can be achieved on the basis of production integration, coordination of national economic plans, and the order of signing foreign trade agreements. The latter ensure that the supply of transferable ruble credits is adequate for the planned volume of trade. Thus plan coordination and the order of signing agreements on mutual deliveries limit the use of the transferable ruble. It can therefore be expected that the monetary functions of the transferable ruble, as opposed to its role as a unit of accounting, will be forced into the background in the coming years.

Accordingly, at present the following characteristics apply to the great majority of CMEA countries and the CMEA international economic system:

a. Trade is regulated by plan coordination and long-term as well as annual intergovernmental trade agreements. The trend is toward reaching agreement on the widest possible range of compulsory export and import quotas.

b. Since the relation between domestic and foreign trade prices is limited, the domestic enterprises do not play an active role in foreign trade. Direct cooperation between enterprises has no defined place within the system.

c. Foreign trade prices are based on capitalist world market prices.

d. The economic cooperation system is organized in physical units.

e. Economic relations between the countries are substantially influenced by the effort to achieve equal bilateral annual trade flows.

f. Factor flows among the countries are calculated in physical units in target programs, particularly in the production of raw materials.

I will consider only the problems of the functions of money related to production integration, monetary policy strategy, its effect on the integration of production, and in general, the interest factors and mechanism for the creation of production integration. However, I do not want to commit the error of assuming that if the problems of market and money relations were solved, the way would be open for a large-scale development of production integration. It is my position that development strategies related to production integration can only be formulated in harmony with the basic concept of integration and on the basis of the corresponding model for planning cooperation. Market and money relations can hinder or promote the development of integration within this framework.

2. The Effect of Monetary Policy on Production Integration

The international financial and settlement system of the socialist countries is part and parcel of the established international economic mechanism, although it developed under different economic and political conditions. This mechanism operates in the context of international economic cooperation between sovereign member countries with centrally planned economic systems. The national economies engaged in this economic cooperation are usually characterized by central planning, administrative directives, and control and finance of production and investment. We can thus say that the international financial and settlement system of the CMEA is a product of the extensive development of the economies.

In the next few years we expect that independent development of the national economies of the member countries will continue to be reflected in the growth of mutual trade and in changes in its pattern. Trade's stagnant growth rates, its lag behind the growth of production, its relatively unchanged pattern, and its slow growth as a percentage of world trade will be reflected in difficulties of transition to intensive development of the economies and of international specialization. There will also be continuing shortages of modern, quality products and a surplus of obsolete, low-quality products on the socialist market for machinery.

The prevailing international economic model does not require the coordination of investment plans, and thus international specialization lags behind the development of planning in the national economies. Thus countries continue to aim for balance-of-payment surpluses. This strategy continues to be embodied in the excessively detailed stipulation of deliveries by a centrally determined quota system that in some cases disregards quality requirements.

It is a common feature of monetary policy in all socialist countries that demand and supply are balanced through the foreign exchange and credit plans of the central banks and the financial organs.

Apart from minor changes the Soviet Union continues to follow the domestic monetary policy it developed when it was an isolated socialist country. The other socialist countries also eliminated the economic functions of exchange rates after World War II and still follow this policy. Thus socialist countries tend to follow isolationist monetary policies developed under specific historical conditions. These policies will probably be followed for the next several years as well.

Finally, domestic monetary policies followed by the CMEA countries in recent years have not aimed at creating a union

The Future of Socialist Economic Integration

between the monetary system and production. The common strategy, rather, has been to keep the international movement of factors of production within precisely determined, narrow limits. In general only factors like capital goods, raw materials, energy, fuel, etc., are moved. Thus the aim of monetary policy can be characterized as securing extensive economic growth without compelling the CMEA countries to coordinate their monetary and fiscal policies. A basic feature of monetary-policy strategy is that it is the communist and workers' parties of the individual countries that are responsible for economic development, rising living standards, and social policy in the countries. It is thus not permissible for an international organization to have a say in these three matters or to affect them through international monetary policy instruments. Because responsibility for these matters will continue to lie with these parties in the coming years, this factor will shape the strategy of monetary policy.

To summarize, the strategy of monetary policy in the CMEA consists of isolated domestic monetary policies linked by arrangements for trade settlements. Domestic regulations eliminate the economic functions of money in every country, and domestic monetary management is isolated from other countries. Thus the national currencies cannot play a role in international trade. They appear only in invisibles; but in terms of our main conclusions, this is an area that can be disregarded.

We now have to determine what the reasons were for this monetary policy strategy's being the main factor in determining the international monetary system of the CMEA for more than twenty-five years. We must also predict whether any changes can be expected in the coming years.

The question must be divided into two parts. With respect to economic and financial potential, the case of the USSR has to be treated separately. The economy of the Soviet Union is the determining factor in mutual economic relations because it has the greatest economic and commercial potential. Thus the USSR plays a decisive role in the system of international pay-

Pricing, Market, and Monetary Relations

ments from the monetary point of view as well. It has vast natural resources and a diversified industrial structure; it is capable of large investments; its internal resources can easily be redeployed; its economies of scale can be fully exploited; it is highly resistant to world economic fluctuations; and in certain areas, e.g., with respect to certain raw materials as well as from the monetary point of view, it is capable of influencing world markets. The new developments in the world economy can only strengthen the potential of the Soviet Union.

In view of the fact that the Soviet Union can develop its economy and solve the problems of its economic growth basically by relying on its own resources, its strategy with respect to monetary policy is mainly politically motivated. This is also true because present international monetary policy strategy — since it concentrates exclusively on setting trade accounts — rules out setting up an international mechanism that would directly influence enterprises' decision-making.

Another aspect of the problem is whether an isolated monetary policy is adequate for the other CMEA countries belonging to the transferable ruble area. There is every indication that in the last twenty-five years this strategy was acceptable for the small countries. But things may be different in the future. If an isolated monetary policy persists, it may create difficulties for the development of integration due mainly to the fact that the functions of money are suppressed.

Thus the isolated monetary policy strategy embodied in the present system generally satisfied the economic interests of both the Soviet Union and the other CMEA countries until now. It corresponded to the level of commodity supply and demand on CMEA markets and influenced them to the desired extent; the system conformed to the directive planning systems; and finally, it allowed each country to pursue policies on the convertible currency markets suited to its national interests.

It is thus clear that if the present concept of integration remains unchanged, no major change can be anticipated in monetary policy strategy in the next few years.

The Future of Socialist Economic Integration

3. The Development of the Settlements System in Production Integration

An analysis of monetary policy strategy clearly leads to the conclusion that we can expect the system of payments within the CMEA to remain unchanged in the coming years. The only change could be expected from the creation of some form of external, limited convertibility for the national currency of the Soviet Union, the ruble. I consider the establishment of a mutual settlements system based on some combination of national currencies and the transferable ruble to be almost out of the question for the period under consideration.

Studies to date have clearly shown that a common currency, based on the directive planning system, complete national sovereignty, increased trade, and the flow of factors of production on a physical basis, can only be a strictly closed unit of accounts. This obviously conflicts with the most elementary requirements of monetary integration. It would therefore appear that in the future, the CMEA monetary system will be differentiated. On the one hand, existing positive elements must be reinforced, and on the other, potential reserves in the present settlements system must be used to their advantage.

With these factors in mind, we shall examine the potential for the development of an international monetary system for the socialist countries from four points of view.

First. The present settlement system still offers possibilities for the future development of trade financing. The accounting system could be changed, perhaps, without further increasing restrictive credit practices. In addition we should strive for multilateral clearing accounts in order to eliminate barriers to foreign trade. The position adopted by the countries on credit and interest related to trade continues to be influenced by their trade balances at any point in time.

Second. The financial side of the development of production integration must be seen clearly. I consider the possibility of direct financial contacts between enterprises almost out of the question in the coming period. This means that specialization and cooperation efforts should be based on five-year and annual commodity exchange agreements for countries where compulsory planning systems still exist. This could mean that indirect methods of finance could be gradually eliminated, and direct methods (direct conversion, direct coefficients, etc.) could again come to the fore.

Third. A number of economists have raised the possibility of introducing partial convertibility of the transferable ruble. They reason that trade between the CMEA countries and the developing countries and cooperation with the advanced capitalist countries, as well as a number of internal problems of socialist cooperation, will make this necessary. On a number of occasions in the last decade, the CMEA countries have considered the possibility of extending the transferable ruble area to include other countries. The conditions and forms of participation by other countries in the transferable ruble settlement area have been formulated, and the countries with which these settlements could be organized have been named. However, the settlement system has not yet succeeded in stimulating the interest of third countries in settling their accounts in transferable rubles.

In my opinion partial convertibility of the transferable ruble cannot be expected within the next ten years. In the first place, the management of a common currency would call for a different concept of integration. Moreover, the creation of a convertible currency on the basis of unanimous support and sovereignty is not possible under the present international financial system. The conditions will not be created for multilateral settlement of debts and credits arising through trade with third countries, particularly the developing countries. The point also has been made that partners using such a currency must respect several conditions in keeping with the rules of the international financial system that ensure mutual advantages in monetary operations over the long run. Finally, the planning conditions and the conditions for the functioning of the exchange rate needed for the operation of such a currency do not exist. In sum, convertibility is unlikely in the coming years, for it is not compatible with the basic concepts of CMEA integration.

Fourth. Creation of restricted external convertibility of the

The Future of Socialist Economic Integration

Soviet ruble could raise other problems for production integration. Convertibility of the national currency of the Soviet Union could make it possible to overcome the financial problems of East-West cooperation, but it could also become an instrument for gradually hardening the conditions of the payments system within the CMEA.

In essence the idea is that the Soviet Union and other socialist countries wanting to do so would sell a given and increasing part of their exports for convertible rubles. This would involve a corresponding change in Soviet accounting and deposit operations conducted with capitalist banks.

The achievement of external convertibility of the Soviet ruble on such a basis could make it possible to formulate a suitable monetary policy in trade and international credit operations, but it would also make it unnecessary for the Soviet Union to adapt its internal economy to the requirements set by the international system of payments. The achievement of a convertibility of this type would present a great opportunity for the smaller socialist countries to reform the operation of their domestic economic systems and to create their own convertible national currencies, even if the present system continues more or less unchanged.

Finally, if the ruble is made convertible, each of the CMEA countries would be able to make its payments in convertible rubles depending on its interests. The direct effect of these payments on production integration could be expressed — particularly in the case of the smaller CMEA countries — in the intensification of production specialization and cooperation potentials offering sales opportunities on more markets, which would ultimately favorably influence production integration by stiffening quality requirements.

4. Price Formation in the CMEA and Its Effect on Exchange Rate Policies

The principles of CMEA price formation are important pil-

Pricing, Market, and Monetary Relations

lars in the institutional system of integration. Along with monetary relations, they directly influence the efficiency of cooperation.

In recent years and in the foreseeable future, two main trends in pricing have been and will continue to be in the foreground of community interest. One is the development and improvement of the traditional and present system of pricing in transferable rubles, which relies on prices on the capitalist world market. The other idea — with several variants — would use the domestic prices of the member countries for fixing international prices, mainly in implementing specialization and cooperation, converting them to transferable rubles by means of a fixed rate of exchange (coefficient) between the national currencies and the transferable ruble.

Owing to the price explosion on the capitalist markets in the midseventies, transferable ruble prices are now revised annually using a "moving average" of capitalist market prices from the preceding five years. We also know that in 1976 the revision of the gold content of the transferable ruble began. This is likely to lead to a situation in which, in order to avoid importing capitalist inflation, the transferable ruble will be frequently revalued against the main capitalist currencies.

This change to a system in which prices are more flexible and change more often means that movements in world market prices can be followed faster and more effectively than with the earlier method of having five-year intervals between changes. Thus the price system works toward effective, more rapid adoption of capitalist world market prices. However, under this system the price level is not as stable as it was before. To some extent this makes foreign trade planning more difficult in countries that use plan directives, and it makes stable planning hard to attain.

According to calculations made a few years ago, between 1980 and 1985 CMEA foreign trade prices may equal capitalist world market prices. On that basis by 1985 we might have shifted to readjusting CMEA prices to capitalist world market prices annually. However, the new 1979-80 price explosion has

Advantages	Disadvantages
Variant I: "Moving Average" Prices	
1. Serves as a shock absorber against the influence of sharp world price changes on the internal formation of prices within a country	1. Signifies the retention of a noneconomic approach to the production problems of cooperation
2. Allows for gradual accommodation to new conditions	2. Balance of mutual payments is great and does not differ substantially from that under the third variant
3. Better approximates real price relationships in world trade (than does the second variant)	3. Preserves the limitation of the hard currency factor in the development of cooperation
4. Some stability and correlation with planning the organizational side of mutual trade	4. Preserves the "naturalization" of mutual trade
5. Compromise form of satisfying the mutual needs of creditors and debtors	5. Conditions created for a lag between the dynamics of contracted and world prices; possibility of price divergence by phases
6. Easier structural adaptation to changing external conditions by national factors and internal mechanisms	6. Promotes the preservation of a dual-stage price system in separate national economies
	7. Price is an insufficient stimulus to technical progress
	8. Weakens the demand for quality

Variant II: "Stop" Prices

1. Serves as a buffer protecting against the influence of external inflation

2. Stability makes long-term planning easier and encourages the organization of noneconomic ties

3. Accommodates the multifaceted organization of the production network and eases changes and reorganizations of the economy

4. No problem with depreciation of the transferable ruble

5. Lessens the importance of imbalances in mutual payments

1. Expresses obsolete technical-economic requirements

2. Accustoms industry to a guaranteed price level and fails to accommodate the modernization of production

3. Weakens the demand for quality

4. Total divergence between the dynamics of world and contractual prices

5. Preserves dual price system

6. Excludes the role of the hard currency factor in the development of integration

7. Significant "naturalization" of exchange

Advantages	Disadvantages
Variant III: "Current World Market" Prices	
1. Stimulates technical progress	1. Stronger import of inflation when compared to the first and second variants
2. Raises the degree of economic approach in production integration and decision-making	2. Changes the concept of stability
3. Provides objective criteria for decision-making	3. Possible reduction in commodity trade resulting from difficulties in marketing low-quality goods
4. Raises industrial demands	4. Growth in the imbalance of mutual payments in comparison with the first and second variants
5. Raises quality demands in production volume on the CMEA market	5. Possibly promotes significant changes in the trade structure
6. Weakens dual-stage pricing	
7. Strengthens the effect of integrating factors resulting from the liquidation of basic price and hard currency discrimination between various goods	
8. Lessens "naturalization" and bilateralism	
9. Creates conditions for an active role for the hard-currency-financing mechanism	

Source: K. Pécsi, "Nekotorye problemy ustanovleniia tsen vo vzaimnoi torgovle," *Tribuna ekonomista mezhdunarodnika* (Moscow), September 1979, p. 100.

changed this forecast. If no further significant price changes occur during the next few years, then it is possible that between 1985 and 1990, CMEA foreign trade prices may come to equal capitalist world market prices, in which case the CMEA might shift to a current world market price base. However, in this way changes would be left to chance. The same result could also be achieved deliberately. But in order to make such a decision on an informed basis, one would have to see clearly the advantages and disadvantages of the three main alternative methods of price formation: the "moving average" method currently used, "stop prices," and contractual prices based on "current world market prices."

A "moving average" price is a price based on relative world market prices from the preceding three to five years. The "stop price" system establishes prices for five years based on average world prices of, say, 1976-80 or only of 1980. Prices based on "current world market" have several variants. For example, contractual prices for a year can be based on average world price for the preceding year or prices based on current world prices on the day the intra-CMEA price is set. Variants falling between these two methods are, of course, also possible.

The advantages and disadvantages of the three main methods are shown in the chart on pages 98-100.[3]

At the beginning of 1980 the Executive Committee of the CMEA decided to maintain without any change the moving average price base for the 1981-85 plan period.

Prices based on a moving average lend a new shape to the exchange-rate policy for the transferable ruble. The "new" exchange-rate policy for the transferable ruble may acquire definite importance with respect to integration, and an appropriate way of handling it may emerge. With exchange rates developing in the member countries under actual efficiency conditions, the rates of exchange between the national currencies and the transferable ruble (or coefficients) may represent a tool of growing importance in generating foreign trade efficiency. The volume of profitable exports and imports at any moment will then increasingly depend on this rate (and in some systems on the rate of exchange or coefficient between the national currency and the dollar). Therefore, in terms of attaining the volume of trade needed for integration, it is likely to become important to coordinate these exchange rates internationally and to handle them within the community centrally. Insofar as the "buyer price principle" as well as the "seller price principle" play some role in practice, collective control of exchange rates may become an important tool in securing relatively low export prices in transferable rubles.

Should this take place, the transferable ruble may become a cornerstone of integration in the context of prices based on a "moving average."

5. Production Integration and National Economic Systems

Up to this point we have examined the effect of market and monetary relations on production integration in the context of monetary policy and export pricing and settlements, that is, in the context of the external components of the CMEA international economic system. But we must also examine the impact of market and monetary relations on domestic economic systems and domestic management systems. It is important to see to what extent these systems promote the cooperation of enterprises in other member countries with Hungarian firms through production integration agreements or through joint companies. It is also necessary to examine how domestic economic systems of the partner countries are coordinated with the CMEA international economic mechanism. We must see to what extent the international CMEA mechanism promotes integration and when integration is promoted by the domestic systems of member countries.

We will examine in terms of market and monetary relationships those elements of planning that can play a role in integration efforts. They are: the directive nature of planning, economic control through economic levers, markets as a means of allocating factors, the profit motive, and the domestic price

Pricing, Market, and Monetary Relations

system. These factors determine the possible set of decisions and the types of relationships on whose basis the demands of the countries participating in production integration can find a common denominator. In order to find this common denominator in production integration, Hungarian government bodies and enterprises contact the government organs and enterprises of the partner countries. It is therefore indispensable for them to know the systems of their partner countries and to analyze the integration method's effect on the development of relationships.

In this context the reform of internal planning and control in the USSR is of greatest importance. It was decided that the role of central planning in the Soviet economy has to change: the main role of planning has to be the formation of medium- and long-term plans. Central planning and disaggregation of plans have to be performed on the basis of scientifically based norms. Enterprises and combines are issued fewer obligatory plan targets than before, and delivery contracts play a much bigger role in relations between firms.

However, the main thrust of the activities of enterprises and combines is determined by the obligatory plan (output, supplies, sales, profitability, etc.). In foreign trade the reform of the control system has yielded few practical changes. Export and import targets are invariably obligatory for the enterprises and combines. Nor has there been any change in the regulations for export and import pricing. This means that export and import prices are adjusted, and thus the effects of foreign trade prices are not transmitted to domestic producers.

Thus in the Soviet economy external effects have been neutralized by setting compulsory export-import targets and by the pricing system. External market impulses are at most disturbances that have to be overcome. Foreign trade can play a role in the economy only to the extent that it is taken into account when the final demands of the economy are established in forming input-output tables. Thus the decisions of central planners are still needed for interenterprise relationships as well as for production integration. In this system enterprises can best

The Future of Socialist Economic Integration

integrate with similar firms in similar systems.

The other CMEA countries introduced other new elements into their economic systems. They assigned some economic decisions to different levels of command. This was done so that the targets set by the central planning agencies, which take the form of instructions, are properly implemented further down the line.

In view of the above a common tendency can be found in the economic reforms of the CMEA countries: they want the role of medium- and long-term planning to grow. The lack of a link between domestic and foreign prices has remained, together with central planning and centralization in foreign trade. The profit motive has a different role in each of the systems. In several cases we find that instead of maximizing profits, the goal is to minimize costs.

Beyond the above, two other points should be separately stressed.

One is that measurement of profitability and efficiency varies widely between the different economic systems of the CMEA countries. The profitability now calculated really indicates little in itself, since it is too closely linked to national biases. The reason for this is that there are essential differences in the pricing and planning systems of the CMEA member countries. Labor productivity, capital intensity, and the efficiency of investments are computed differently, reflecting the requirements of the planning systems. There are also differences in accounting methods and in prices. In many cases, as in Hungary, cooperation — even domestic — is hindered by the system of taxation. As a result the industries of the member countries have in many cases few chances to explore and coordinate their own interests in international specialization and production integration.

Production integration is considerably influenced by the protectionistic measures applied in the CMEA countries. Some of these measures are subsidies, conversion coefficients, the present system of accounting foreign exchange, foreign exchange allocations for imports, and investment limits. Thus the enterprises are, in general, not sufficiently stimulated to participate in production integration, particularly in cooperation.

The second factor concerns direct contacts between enterprises. The fact that a place for these contacts has not yet been found in the system of cooperation also requires explanation.

In some member countries even now, enterprises are not empowered to establish direct relationships with enterprises in other countries or to enter into contracts. When reforming their economic systems, the member countries could not yet deal with such contacts, and thus some elements in these systems hinder interenterprise relations.

These factors blocking integration should be seen as realities, as concrete conditions existing in the individual countries. Thus, while in most member countries a system of directive central planning now functions, its future survival must also be considered. This means that the controlled market environment needed for true expansion of production integration and for its union with market integration cannot be expected in every country, and this in turn permits only gradual implementation of production integration.

The dilemma for Hungary stems from the fact that during our economic reform, we transferred interests related to the implementation of production integration partially to the enterprise sphere. Decisions on international production integration, cooperation, and international economic unions are made on the basis of enterprise interests. But the economic systems of the partner countries are more conducive to integration conducted on the governmental level, where production and exports fit into the production, material and technical supply, investment, and foreign trade sections of the national economic plan as instructions.

When we elaborated our economic reform, the problem of how to incorporate production integration into it had not yet emerged. We relied on the experience that economic reforms are not implemented in the CMEA countries with the same intensity or at the same rate. We assumed there would be other countries in which increasing enterprise efficiency, the profit motive, the linking of domestic and foreign prices with economic instruments, increasing the information value of domestic prices, and market elements in general would be introduced into the system of economic control. These countries would also have to adapt to their partners sooner or later. This assumption has not proved true. The preservation of directive economic planning and its effect on production integration will be realities for a long time to come.

This suggests that steps to coordinate Hungary's economic mechanism with the directive planning systems of the other countries will depend primarily on measures taken by the Hungarians themselves. We must clearly perceive the place and role of the forms of production integration, cooperation, and joint enterprises promoted by the state and based on enterprise interests. Then we will have to take measures that stress the role of government intervention, influence, and control in the field of production integration in order to adapt to the control systems of our partner countries. The extent of adaptation will be influenced by our perceived interests.

Thus in terms of the effect of market and money relationships on domestic economic systems, it is likely that production integration will develop gradually.

The development of production integration and joint enterprises is also blocked by the prevailing system of monetary and financial cooperation as well as by other methods applied in cooperation. It is also clear that the preconditions for direct contacts entailing the development of production integration are brought about by further improvement of economic systems and of the integration process, particularly improvements in monetary, financial, foreign trade, and price relations. On the other hand, greater integration assures a larger role for these relations.

The present socialist international trade and financial systems came into existence on the basis of the principles of directive planning, and the only objective reason for a change in them would be a trend toward reforming this system of planning. On this basis we can predict that economic cooperation in the coming years will be a process of laying the foundations of integration by influencing economic policy, plan coordination, foreign trade, and financial activities. We can expect only limited progress in eliminating difficulties in and obstacles to production integration, and particularly cooperation based on enterprise interests, caused by the international economic system. Elimination of these obstacles and the creation of new conditions can be expected only in the next one or two five-year plan periods. We must face this fact and the need for gradualness when formulating our strategy for production integration.

Economic changes directed at developing production integration are possible to the extent that they strengthen and do not weaken the power and unity of the socialist community, politically as well as economically. Under these circumstances socialist international production integration and the further development of its institutions can be expected to take place in a number of stages under the alternating influence of economic compulsion and political activity.

6. Theoretical Aspects of Price Formation in Specialization and Cooperation

We have already surveyed the problem of foreign trade prices in the CMEA international economic mechanism. However, some hold that other prices, different from those applied in foreign trade, should be used in specialization and cooperation. Here the problem emerges of developing "buyer prices." It has been argued that producing and selling products manufactured through specialization at world market prices does not sufficiently account for the particular features of production cooperation. If prices in specialization agreements were set at world market level, they would not lead to efficiency. Thus, according to this standpoint, in the interest of mutually securing efficiency, products produced through specialization should have prices that are lower than market prices.[4] This would be logical — it is said — because the costs of national production inputs in specialization and in cooperation are lower than prices of identical products on the world market. In addition, it is assumed that the advantages of specialization and cooperation agreements are enjoyed primarily by the producers, and that the latter realize this advantage exclusively through price.

It is worthwhile discussing this problem separately because in some cases, theory has become economic and foreign trade policy. It is well known, e.g., that several price levels have already emerged for exports and imports of Zhiguli cars and parts produced under specialization and cooperation agreements.

One can say in general that the price level of products produced under specialization and cooperation agreements cannot be examined apart from the other elements of trade. The success of these agreements lies precisely in the fact that volume, delivery deadlines, technical parameters, and other conditions of delivery, as well as prices, are simultaneously clarified. A thorough analysis of all these items allows interested parties to evaluate the economic efficiency of the deals and to decide on this basis whether it is expedient to conclude an agreement. Because of differences between the interests of the seller and the buyer, it is correct to assume that the prices of products turned out under specialization and cooperation agreements must correspond to normal foreign trade prices, yet they must be more elastic than the latter. I do not want to deal with the details of this problem but rather would like to point out some of its economic aspects, including those which can influence, enhance, or retard the further development of production integration of the CMEA countries.

As regards the prices of parts and components produced under specialization and cooperation agreements, the methodological implementation of the principle of "buyer price" entails, of course, some special problems. The main problems are, of course, not those of methods but those that stem from the expected conditions under which they are to be applied.

We should first see that if this principle prevails, the uniform system of CMEA prices ceases to be uniform. The ad-

Pricing, Market, and Monetary Relations

herents of this principle also see this clearly. Bautina and Shastitko write:

> It cannot be denied that revising price formation is quite difficult from both the practical and the theoretical standpoints. There is more than one variant, and a series of counterarguments can be advanced against each of them. If in the agreements on specialization and cooperation we deviate from the world market prices applied in commodity exchange as the basis of price formation, this leads to diversification of the prices on the socialist markets with identical products and causes difficulties in normal trade in these products on the socialist world market.[5]

What is this all about? Prices of parts and components produced under specialization and cooperation would be based on the domestic (producer) prices of the member countries. For finished products in which there is specialization and cooperation, the system of prices based on a moving average of prices on capitalist markets has been proposed with shorter periods of fixity, while for other products the usual five-year base period has been proposed. If prices on the capitalist world market stabilized, we might return to a system of contractual prices fixed for periods longer than a year. But when no direct trade in the commodity takes place on the world market, international prices set on the basis of national costs could be preferred.

This set of proposals is not consistent with the correct system of CMEA pricing, which sets prices exclusively on the basis of those on the world market. Application of national price bases would create a situation in which specific regional prices would be disadvantageous either for the exporters or for the importers relative to the prices obtainable on the world market. This might lead to a deline in intra-CMEA trade under cooperation agreements.

This is so grave a counterargument that it merits detailed examination.

From the theoretical standpoint it seems quite natural to include the national price (cost) level in the system of international price formation, so that each national producer can try to realize its actual costs and intended profits in international trade. But this claim is justified only to the extent that the producer has a real chance — deriving from the system of domestic management and price formation — to claim actual costs and intended profit domestically. A price system with fixed prices is typically a price system in which there is no place for this. In such price systems the mechanism linking the producer to export markets ensures that the producer is not obligated to cover actual costs on these markets.

Thus in my opinion this proposal is basically wrong. Behind every such theory we find the inconsistency that domestic prices are compared to world market prices and, through them, to the domestic prices of another country, even though the two domestic prices and the world market price are not linked by an actually operating rate of exchange. Therefore the pricing of parts and components to be produced under cooperation and specialization agreements must not be based on national producer prices.

Producer prices in the CMEA countries do not uniformly express total social labor inputs in the given products. These prices can substantially differ from each other by countries, industries, and products. The particular features of the price systems are of course linked to those of the financial systems. In establishing the producer prices of the different groups of products, economic policy considerations that differ by countries play a role. Differences also arise from the national features of the system of cost accounting. The dates when fixed assets were revalued are different, as are the depreciation rates and the taxes levied on wages. Furthermore import prices, particularly in the countries strongly dependent on imports, influence both production costs and producer prices. Finally, production specialization and cooperation in identical products differ from country to country, and thus the profit content of prices is also different. Because profit is usually projected into costs by phases of production, the cumulation of profits similarly differs by countries. Thus the statement does not hold that after conversion of national producer prices to the foreign trade price level by means of an internal coefficient, the countries participating in cooperation would be compensated for their production inputs. At present, producer prices do not consistently reflect actual inputs.

Therefore, if we assume domestic price systems isolated from world market prices and the lack of a rate of exchange that would orient production costs constantly toward the world market level, production integration relations might suffer not only in cooperation aimed at parts and components but also in specialization in finished products.

Moreover the application of the world market pricing principle to finished products and that of domestic cost bases in cooperation covering parts and components creates a new situation in exchange rate policy.

A new factor in exchange rate policy inevitably emerges if a considerable part of trade is made up of products whose price is determined by national price bases, thereby creating a transferable ruble that originates on a basis other than the capitalist price base and is of a different value.

The emergence of "new" transferable rubles is an unavoidable consequence of a change in the pricing principle. Let us consider an illustrative example.

Suppose a country has exports worth 2,000 transferable rubles based on capitalist prices. After the introduction of pricing based on domestic costs, half of its exports will remain on the capitalist price basis and thus be worth 1,000 transferable rubles. But the other half will be priced using domestic prices and will be worth, say, 500 transferable rubles in view of the exchange rate of the buyer's national currency to the transferable ruble and its domestic price level. Then in the trade of the exporter two kinds of transferable rubles with quite different price levels will appear. This is also shown by the fact that it can transact the second half of its trade in a profitable way if for the second kind of transferable ruble the exchange rate is set at twice the "traditional" transferable ruble rate. It should be obvious that one "kind" of 1,000 transferable rubles and the other "kind" of 500 transferable rubles cannot be simply added up as claims arising from exports because they are not claims of the same real value; thus they have to be recorded separately. The situation is somewhat different in the case of the "seller price base," that is, when the basis of the price formation in terms of transferable rubles is the national price of the seller. If in the exporter country the exchange rate of the transferable ruble based on capitalist prices is operative, the country can use it in setting the export price. In this case the level of the export price in transferable rubles as a starting point will be identical on a domestic price basis with the transferable ruble price established on a capitalist price basis. It is, however, most likely that the two kinds of price level will sooner or later drift farther apart, and the aggregation problem will also arise here.

The simultaneous operation of the two principles does not seem farfetched, and the experts quoted also assume parallel operation. But even so, we cannot be sure that every member country will find it possible to form prices on a domestic basis for every other member.

The "new" transferable rubles will differ — in the best case — only by countries, i.e., when every country is capable of determining a uniform rate of exchange for its productive sphere. If there is no such possibility, the rates of exchange must be established by industries. In any case there will be as many exchange rates (conversion coefficients) of national currencies to the transferable ruble as countries officially declare. And they will define as many kinds of transferable rubles as the directions in which the trade they transact differs in value from value measured in terms of the nominal transferable ruble.

In this context one of the problems to be resolved is how to add the different kinds of transferable rubles. Problems of multilaterality may become more complicated if a rate of exchange declared by some member country proves to be unrealistic for another, and therefore, when making commercial agreements or enforcing trade policy intentions, it applies a premium or discount to the rate of exchange in question — either openly or covertly.

Nevertheless the basic problems of multilateralism change little because of the appearance of a transferable ruble based on national price systems. The "multilateralization" of bilateral balances and resolution of the confrontation of groups of products with groups of products will cause the same troubles as under world market pricing. The difference between the present situation and that perhaps emerging will rather be that today the statement of the real value of bilateral balances in transferable rubles would cause trouble, while with a national price basis, the statement of realistic rates of exchange of the national currencies to the transferable rubles would do so. Ultimately the two problems are related.

A few practical problems directly affecting the development of production integration also merit closer attention.

The first problem is that if prices of parts and components produced under cooperation are based on cost of domestic inputs, enterprise-level inputs become the starting points for pricing. This leads to a logical contradiction because under the present concept of production integration, direct cooperation between enterprises is impossible, while prices for these products (parts and components) are based on the costs of the enterprise.

The domestic price system in the concrete form of buyer (importer) prices is particularly suited to redistributing profits among countries through the foreign trade price. But in terms of economic policy — and thus of integration — it is not expedient to redistribute income through foreign trade prices to enterprises in a decentralized way and thus without central control. This highly important process should be kept in central channels.

Next we should point out that insofar as we rely on two kinds of price bases with respect to parts produced under cooperation, two possibilities emerge. One is that the price of the part or component is lower than its world market price. In this case, e.g., in an enterprise using a great deal of imported ma-

The Future of Socialist Economic Integration

terial, the contradiction emerges that it gets its imported raw materials, fuel, and energy at world market prices, while it exports the product made from them at a price corresponding to the domestic cost of inputs of the buyer. The practical implications of the difference between the two prices should be obvious.

Nor does the contrary case — that is, when product prices considerably exceed the world market price — promote production integration. Let us look at the following actual example.[6]

At one time electronic pocket calculators were scarce in Hungary. When Bulgaria started producing them, we imported Bulgarian calculators at a price of over 100 rubles. The domestic consumer price was between 5,000 and 6,000 Ft [$250-$300]. Given this high consumer price, a Hungarian firm also tried to produce such calculators; but the import contents alone amounted to $15, not to mention the cost of labor and domestic materials used. Since the pressure of domestic demand for cheaper pocket calculators was great, to reduce its price the Hungarian foreign trade company imported calculators from Hong Kong which for $15 matched or even exceeded the quality of the Bulgarian calculators. Of course, the import of Bulgarian calculators, with their unrealistic price, ceased. Import of Soviet pocket calculators appears possible in two years, but they too are likely to have high prices.

It can thus be seen that unrealistically high CMEA foreign trade prices hamper CMEA production integration.

Considering all this, there remains no other way out of this fix than to determine the prices of the products to be produced under cooperation and specialization agreements by relying on the prevailing world market prices. This principle is theoretically better than using domestic producer prices as the basis even when there is no link between the producer price and the world market price level. The socialist world market price is the monetary expression of the international value of the commodity, and its size is determined by the necessary labor inputs on the world market. This does not, of course, exclude the possibility that the sales price established for products to be produced under specialization and cooperation, by approximating international prices, will be advantageous for every participant. Obviously it is expedient to set up specialized production where natural conditions, technological equipment, and production experience are most advantageous. But productivity requirements that accord with world market prices must be absolutely reckoned with, and deviation from them is justified only in exceptional cases (production of scarce articles, industrial development in the economically underdeveloped socialist countries, etc.).

It is very important to remember that the problem can be solved only by unifying production and market integration through uniform exchange rates within the CMEA that permit the comparison of prices expressed in a uniform currency. A uniform rate of exchange will provide a comparative basis for computing the efficiency indicators that help in selecting the most efficient investments. Uniform exchange rates should permit producers to judge the profitability of exports and compare domestic inputs with the value received in foreign exchange. They should also serve as an instrument for settlements among the socialist countries.

For the time being, for lack of favorable conditions, we cannot establish a uniform rate of exchange equally suited to economic analysis, to pricing of products to be produced under specialization and cooperation, to the examination of the efficiency of foreign trade, and to accounting and settlements. It follows that for some time it will still be necessary to maintain a system of multiple rates of exchange (or coefficients).

This situation demands that we solve as soon as possible a number of currency conversion problems entailed in the examination of production under specialization and cooperation by taking into account world market prices. From this it may follow that the profitability of such transactions should be seen and evaluated by each country only within its own national system of valuation. If we intolerantly and unrealistically shift to the "buyer" pricing principle, which deviates from the world market pricing principle, the development of CMEA production integration may come to a halt in certain cases.

The way out certainly leads through the unity of production and market integration, that is, through linking the domestic price systems of the CMEA countries with the world market price system and through applying the efficiency, quality, and technological requirements of the world market to the domestic requirements of the member countries.

One other factor should be taken into account. The production of parts and components under cooperation may require new approaches to price bargaining.

One such approach can be that in all cases in which additional efficiency accrues from specialized and cooperative production of parts and components, the participating parties may grant each other certain preferences, as in the usual determination of world market prices. But only world market prices can serve as a basis for this, and the purpose of the whole can only be to attain world standards with respect to the greatest possible number of products.

It is also possible to use the buyer's domestic prices when the export price in transferable rubles is set by the domestic price of the buyer, if it is not lower than the price obtained by the exporter with identical or similar exports to the capitalist countries. Thus the price of exports to the socialist countries would be determined by the higher of the two, i.e., the price of exports to capitalist countries or the domestic price of the buyer.

This principle would ensure, on the one hand, that the domestic price level of the buyer would be taken into account (and if there are no exports of this article to the West, this would determine the export price), while on the other hand, it would prevent the socialist export price from becoming disadvantageous and trade and production integration from declining with respect to products exported to both main markets. The price levels thus developing for the individual countries would probably not be more disadvantageous than those outlined earlier, provided that exports to the CMEA countries consisted mostly of products also exported to the capitalist countries.

Pricing, Market, and Monetary Relations

7. International Investment Problems Due to CMEA Monetary Relations

Some economists and researchers have justified investment in the development of sources of raw materials by saying that they are needed because world market prices do not cover production costs, and producers of raw materials therefore have no incentive to develop production. This is so general, well-known, and widely held an opinion among economists that I do not intend to argue it in detail. Let us consider, for example, an opinion expressed at a scholarly conference held in 1971: "The credit form of contribution by the CMEA countries," stresses the author,

> to some extent increases the material interest of the Soviet Union in the development of production of raw materials and fuels. It should be taken into account that current contract prices for fuels and raw materials are so low that in the majority of cases, they do not cover average production costs in the extractive branches, to say nothing of economic rent. Raising the present contract prices for a number of fuels and raw materials could therefore be an incentive in solving the raw material and fuel problem.[7]

It is well known that in the period from 1958 to 1972, the change in the average world market price level did not exceed 2% a year. However, the price explosion of 1973-74 brought a fundamental change: an acceleration in the world market price changes. While raw material prices rose only 14% over the level for 1952-56 until the end of 1972, in 1973 they doubled in a single year; and crude oil prices, for example, rose four or five times. Changes in the relative prices and terms of trade for raw materials and finished products in favor of raw material and energy also contributed to this extremely large price change. Large price movements and shifts in relative prices created a gap between earlier contract prices and current prices. The world market price of energy sources is expected to remain high.

This price development in itself would justify the need to review the previous position. A country making investments for the development of raw materials production can now be compensated for the expenditures it makes through foreign trade prices that exceed the previous capitalist world market prices. The higher interest charges on the credits to finance investments in raw materials production can also be easily covered from the higher prices.

However, the question of incentive prices is only one, although an important side, of the matter. What I consider more important is the justification for and theoretical soundness of investment contributions taking into account prices, credits, financial interrelations, and the question of interest.

As a starting point we must take into account the fact that in our system of cooperation, long-term credits have assumed the nature of intergovernmental and, in a number of cases, general aid. In these cases the credit conditions — a low interest rate and generally a maturity of ten years — have departed from the requirement of a balance of credit needs and sources. Under the present credit system the readiness of certain countries to extend loans is underestimated, while the capacity of others to borrow is overestimated. The use of different categories is not exploited in the interest of shifting to an intensive stage of integration; and as a result of the limitations on the monetary functions of the transferable ruble, the effect of excessively centralized economic control systems is felt in the credit system. This emerges in two different effects. One is that instead of financing trade or development programs, credit operations are used to offset overall imbalances provided for in the national plans or arising unexpectedly in the course of plan implementation. The other is that long-term credits are not necessarily granted for the soundest credit needs. Credit related to investment contributions is a relevant example.

There is a genuine need for credit. However, the problem with credit in the present system stems from the present way of pricing exports. We use prices derived from the capitalist world market. However, we do not follow this logic consistently. We use world market prices, but price is only one factor in economic relations on the world market. As the expression of international value, it embraces a series of components. They include a complicated system of sales conditions, modes of payment, credit, and preferences related to price. Thus in view of the fact that prices are derived from the capitalist world market, where credit is not related to raw material imports, a contradiction arises in our system of economic cooperation by our adopting the world market price but not the conditions that shape it, and by our making economic decisions on the basis of a price formed in this way.

The essence of the problem is that credit on the world market is basically extended for machinery exports. The costs of credit are covered by the machinery exporter, and this is reflected accordingly in the price. However, in our settlement system price is not related to the conditions of credit and payment. We adopt world market machinery export prices, but we do not extend credits related to the sale of machinery. This has a twofold effect. On the one hand, genuine credit needs related to price in the machinery-importing and raw-material-exporting countries are not covered. On the other hand, in the machinery-exporting and raw-material-importing countries, efficiency calculations made using foreign trade prices based on the capitalist market provide a much more favorable picture than reality because machinery is exported for cash payment, and the cost of credit related to sales is not reflected in the efficiency calculations. In my opinion it is largely this circumstance that explains why the efficiency of machinery and manufacturing production appears considerably greater than it actually is in the individual national valuation systems.

We must conclude in this context that when we extend credit in the form of investment contributions — and at a high world market price — we are acting erroneously, for it is not here that credit should be extended. I believe that this is one key to the further development of production integration, primarily in

The Future of Socialist Economic Integration

the area of granting credit. I am firmly convinced that we must use foreign trade prices consistently. If we adopt a price — and we now adjust it annually — we cannot ignore the economic conditions under which this price becomes an economically meaningful category.

Finally, in connection with this question the new phenomenon related to the generalization of the problem of investment contributions should be mentioned.

Another and related problem is the extension of credits for target programs. Recently researchers and economists in some CMEA countries have noted the problem that, in general, investment contributions should be made for capacity necessary for additional imports of raw materials and fuels. To quote once again in this context:

> At present, coordination of the national economic plans of the Soviet Union and the other CMEA countries for the 1976-80 period has taken shape and is nearing completion. A new document of principle was adopted at the Twenty-ninth Session of the CMEA (Budapest, 1975) — the countries' coordinated plan of integration measures for the years 1976-80. Work is also being carried out at the same time on the basis of the long-term plan of integration measures necessary for the solution of the production tasks outlined by the Comprehensive Program, taking into account the previously established objectives for development of the Soviet Union's long-term external economic relations: steady reduction of the proportion of products on a low level of processing in Soviet exports; raising the share of machinery and equipment exports to a level corresponding to the country's economic potential; increasing raw material and fuel production only on the basis of the long-term comprehensive economic plans for production involving the investments from the countries concerned; the development of deep and long-term international specialization and cooperation in science, technology, and production.[8]

Pricing, Market, and Monetary Relations

I would like to stress only one idea from the above quotation: I think that an increment in fuel and raw material exports will be provided only within the framework of long-term target programs using investments from the countries concerned. This merits particular attention because it has increasingly become everyday economic policy. It is therefore necessary to consider any problems that might arise from the general adoption of this policy in terms of market and money relations. The seeds of these problems can already be seen.

If target programs are clearly defined and directed at solving one or two major tasks on the basis of the "decisive link" principle, they make it possible to combine resources to reach the goal set. However, if we want to solve all the problems of CMEA cooperation within the framework of target programs, then, by the nature of things, we will not be able to combine and concentrate resources. Obviously, if all tasks get top priority, we actually are giving priority to none. A similar situation can be predicted with regard to the demand outlined in the quotation. If certain CMEA countries believe that an increment in raw material and fuel exports can only be provided against investment contributions, it logically follows that all CMEA countries will correctly hold that raw materials within their export structure can only be exported to the other CMEA countries in return for an investment contribution. It is relatively easy to foresee the related difficulties. However, this is increasingly becoming practice in so-called "construction" deals, when, for example, oil is delivered in exchange for wheat, other raw materials, and so on. If this practice becomes general, the movement toward barter deals in cooperation will intensify and might become a means for further rigidifying the present structure of trade.

Chapter VIII
Problems of Trade Settled in Convertible Currencies among CMEA Member Countries

1. Background to Hard Currency Settlements in Intra-CMEA Trade

Changes in the world economy in the early and midseventies and developments in East-West trade raised new problems for trade and monetary relations among CMEA countries. One of the most important issues was the growth of trade settled in convertible currencies within the region.

Although the monetary and financial mechanism of the CMEA is today a secondary element in production integration, it is an important one. We have seen that it can promote and accelerate cooperation, but it can also impede progress. After the International Bank for Economic Cooperation (IBEC) was set up in the midsixties, followed by the International Investment Bank (IIB), there was a formal shift to multilateral settlements; an international credit mechanism was established; and a collective currency, the transferable ruble, was born.

As noted above, the major problem in this new socialist international monetary system is that the multilateral system of settlements in the CMEA is deficient in several areas. Although we have created a legal framework and the accounting and financial means for multilateral settlements, hardly any progress has been made toward genuine multilateralism. The member countries still try to balance their bilateral trade flows because

Trade and Convertible Currencies

claims on third countries cannot be used to cover a deficit. The problem of efficiently stimulating an increase in the volume of trade has not been solved, nor has the problem of balance-of-payments deficits or surpluses. In recent years several proposals and ideas have emerged. It has become obvious that solving the problem of actual multilateral payments is quite closely related to the improvement of the system of foreign trade agreements, to more trade without quotas, and to other economic policy preconditions, including a comprehensive reform of economic control systems.

This is the general background from which we should understand the proposals and experiments that have been made in the twenty-three years since the first multilateral clearing agreement in 1957 with respect to "hardening" internal settlements and enforcing world market standards on our markets. A hardening of settlement conditions, which ultimately necessitates making internal settlements on the basis of their value in convertible currency and hence integrating settlements into the world market, has several economic and political motives.

The most important economic motive is to eliminate differences between the quality of those commodities traded internally and of those traded on the world market — an economic fact that has been with us since the late fifties.

In intra-CMEA trade, in several cases "soft" goods are no longer acceptable, and commodities that meet the quality requirements of third markets are now demanded. This has prompted an insistence on intra-CMEA trade on even tighter balance between commodities and groups of commodities.

One can see this trend in the preference of CMEA enterprises for exporting to CMEA markets while seeking imports from third markets. (For a limited number of commodities, the opposite is true.) This fact compels the national economic authorities to take various economic and administrative steps to maintain equilibrium in the balance of payments, which again degenerates into contradictory and complicated systems of control.

The increasing international division of labor tends to reduce

The Future of Socialist Economic Integration

differences in quality and productivity between the two markets. A considerable part of the monetary relations between the two markets consists of buy-back agreements (subassemblies, parts, intermediate products, etc.). Because of the differing values of the currencies involved, the efficiency of these operations remains obscure. Their impact on the balance of payments is almost invisible on the microlevel. In several cases this fact creates a disincentive to technological development and improvement of quality.

The possibility of third countries joining the community creates a political motive for hardening trade. The most important issue for every entrant is to secure a suitable means of exchange with CMEA countries.

Finally, in accordance with the concept of peaceful coexistence, integration in the international monetary system is inevitable. Economically this is due to the needs of peaceful economic competition, while politically it stems from the need to enhance the appeal of socialism in monetary and fiscal terms.

Since 1957 a number of very interesting and far-reaching proposals on convertibility and the CMEA settlements systems have been put forward. However, these proposals have not been implemented; or if they were attempted, they ended in failure. This raises several general theoretical and practical problems.

First, until recently interest in increasing the volume of trade and the need to accelerate growth in intra-CMEA trade have predominated.

Second, efficiency and, in this context, the implications of the domestic economic systems for the international financial system have remained in the background.

Third, proposals aimed at solving the problems of pricing, credit, exchange rate policy, and tariffs have been inconsistent. Economic methods to replace the administrative measures that protect national markets and the gradual coordination of these methods in the CMEA while maintaining a planned economy remained undeveloped and were simply not discussed.

Fourth, incentives for export sales and methods to promote trade on each others' markets (modern marketing, etc.) have been neglected. Administrative directives continue to characterize foreign trade.

Fifth, financial integration into the world economic system was seen as a gradual process.

Sixth, our ideas tended toward creation of a common monetary system. Explicitly or implicitly, from the Multilateral Clearing Agreement in 1957 to the latest proposals, we have tried to follow the monetary agreements of the Common Market and, by analogy, of the European Payments Union. In fact we have never developed a socialist alternative.

An evaluation of the tasks facing the CMEA shows that a shift to more efficient CMEA monetary and financial mechanisms and their stage-by-stage implementation have been hard to achieve. It would, however, be a mistake to conclude that the main reason for this is a lack of political determination on the part of CMEA governments. The pressure of inevitable real forces has made it difficult to implement reform plans through the national economic systems of member countries that operate differently.

Hence the idea of permitting conversion of the transferable ruble into convertible currencies is not yet the order of the day; it is a matter for the more distant future.[1] In fact, it would require a radical reorganization of economic institutions. That is why I agree with the economists Petr Chvojka (Czechoslovakia),[2] George Creiniceanu (Romania),[3] and others who advocate a lower, more easily attained level of convertibility of the national currencies. They advocate the creation of a community monetary and financial system that would permit increased utilization of the advantages of multilateral settlements and, ultimately, of the international division of labor and integration into the international financial system while observing our own socialist interests.

2. Estimating the Volume of Intra-CMEA Trade Settled in Convertible Currencies

An empirical investigation of the problem suggests that intra-

The Future of Socialist Economic Integration

CMEA trade in convertible currencies flows through three main channels. The first is direct trade settled in convertible currencies at world market prices. The second is indirect trade settled the same way. The third is credits and investments made in convertible currencies. The availability of statistics varies with respect to these three components.[4]

a. Direct Trade Settled in Convertible
   Currencies within the CMEA

Trade settled directly in convertible currencies has clearly grown since the early seventies. Attempts at estimating its volume, on the basis of official Hungarian data,[5] have been made in the international economic literature.[6] In 1978 an official Hungarian foreign trade communiqué provided information about trade settled in convertible currencies between Hungary and the CMEA countries. Deputy Minister of Foreign Trade Jenő Tordai stated in Világgazdaság [Foreign Trade] (April 7, 1978): "Besides trade with the CMEA countries settled in rubles, the value of transactions now settled in convertible foreign exchange is also substantial.... In 1977 we exported to the CMEA countries commodities valued at $342 million and imported from them $194 million." Moreover, Minister of Foreign Trade József Biró stated in Népszabadság [Financial Matters] (April 23, 1978) that the value of trade transacted with the Soviet Union and settled in convertible currency had reached $330 million in 1977. In 1978 exports to socialist countries for "dollar and other nonruble" settlement currencies decreased slightly, from 28 billion forints to 26 billion forints. Imports rose from 17.5 billion to 19.5 billion forints.[7] If we apply the 1977 forint to dollar exchange rate of 40 forints = $1.00, the dollar equivalents are $700 and $650 million exports in 1977 and 1978 and $438 and $488 million imports in the corresponding years. Socialist countries, of course, encompass a larger group of countries than just the CMEA members.

We can conclude from these figures that in 1977, Hungarian trade within the CMEA settled in convertible currencies amounted to about 8-10% of its total trade with socialist countries. In 1978 it was substantially the same.[8] This raises the question of how to evaluate such trade. Formally commodities exchanged within the CMEA that are settled in convertible currencies are "hard" commodities — goods that can be sold on the world market for convertible currency at normal world market prices. In the literature this is usually rationalized as eliminating middlemen. Supposedly, mutual purchases by CMEA members mediated by capitalist merchants increased after the world market price explosion. But this cannot be proven statistically.[9]

These rationalizations show the doubts about the quantification of advantages from trade accounted in transferable rubles. They also relfect the effects of the CMEA trade system, in which goods are evaluated in physical units and trade is conducted bilaterally, which restricts the rational international division of labor. They show that the current CMEA foreign trade settlement mechanism does not adequately satisfy the trade interests of the commodity producers.

Many consider the emergence of trade settled in convertible currencies a positive development. They see such settlements as an advance for multilateralism in terms of the development of market and money relations within the CMEA. It is also a positive development in the sense that it creates a mutually acceptable way of engaging in trade that was not possible using the transferable ruble. At the same time, it reduces the effect of the traditional bilateralism in trade and finance that restricts mutual trade. Thus settlements in convertible currencies have increased the extent of mutually advantageous international socialist division of labor. They help eliminate the investment contributions tied to some commodities purchased with transferable rubles; but they do strengthen trade in physical units, since instead of linking commodity groups, this exchange links specific kinds of commodities.

As opposed to traditional clearing in transferable rubles, convertible currency trade has the advantage that in the interest of expressing comparative advantages, trade primarily takes place at world market prices and uses world market contractual conditions. Trade in convertible currencies provides the countries with a commonly accepted price. But this positive feature vanishes as soon as more complex manufactured products are traded. Trade in these commodities rarely occurs because of the difficulties in agreeing on prices for these goods. That is why this system cannot be used in all trade. Its appearance, with all its advantages and limitations, is soundly pragmatic. It has successfully eliminated a bottleneck (i.e., the difficulties related to trade in "hard" raw materials), but it is not a theoretical breakthrough.

b. The Import Content of Exports

There is a significant indirect flow of convertible currencies in CMEA internal trade in the form of commodities. Methodo-

Table 5

Changes in the Import Content of Exports in Terms of Value
(1974 as % of 1972 values)
(1972 = 100)

	Import content of			
	exports settled in rubles		exports settled in currencies other than rubles	
	from areas accounted in			
	rubles	currencies other than rubles	rubles	currencies other than rubles
Industrial items	89.3	213.7	143.5	385.1
Agricultural items	91.2	255.4	131.8	444.6
Total economy	90.9	223.1	140.9	367.8

Source: Klára Beke and László Hunyadi, "A magyar export importanyag tartalma," Külgazdaság, 1977, no. 7.

Trade and Convertible Currencies

logical and statistical difficulties make this hard to show empirically. However, some recent computations in Hungary have approached the problem.[10] Some of their results are shown in Table 5.

The figures in Table 5 demonstrate that the nonruble import content of ruble exports doubled in the period examined, while their ruble import content has remained roughly the same. In hard currency exports the ruble import content increased only slightly. These figures also indicate that nonruble import prices evidently increased much faster than did socialist prices, but in 1974 the quantity of inputs imported from capitalist countries in Hungarian exports to both main markets exceeded earlier amounts by several times, mainly in terms of value but

Table 6

Import Content of Exports in 1974
(in %)

	Exports settled in rubles		Exports settled in other currencies	
	imports from areas accounted in			
	rubles	other currencies	rubles	other currencies
Metallurgy	27.55	17.38	17.51	11.05
Engineering	10.75	16.35	9.93	15.10
Chemicals	12.48	33.63	13.23	35.68
Light industry	9.18	35.45	7.90	28.78
Total economy	9.53	20.05	7.35	15.48
Industry total	11.20	25.63	9.50	21.5
Food	6.83	37.18	5.37	28.72
Agriculture	5.85	20.03	3.37	11.55
Agriculture and food	6.33	26.68	4.13	17.38

Source: See Table 5.

also in terms of volume. This trend accelerated and continued through the late 1970s.

Two methods will be used to approach this issue of convertible currency content in trade within the CMEA. First, the input-output analysis cited above will be used, and then we will use figures for machinery imports from the West (including subassemblies and parts).

Let us look at the results of the input-output computations (see Table 6).

Table 6 shows that the hard currency import content of 100 Ft of exports to the socialist countries is 20 Ft, while the ruble import content of exports to the nonruble area is about half that. Distribution by sectors reveals some interesting facts. In ruble exports, investments in the chemical industry and the light and food industries require most of the convertible currencies. Exports from the engineering industry have relatively low hard currency input values, but presumably ruble exports from high-technology industries show a higher hard currency import content.

Let us turn now to imports of machinery, equipment, subassemblies, and parts from nonruble areas (see Table 7).

The figures show a markedly increasing trend.

Moreover, changes in the cumulated import content are also important. These figures show that beyond direct trade in imported materials and parts, machines imported from the West

Table 7

Imports of Machinery, Vehicles, and Other Investment Goods Settled in Dollars, at Current Prices

	1971	1972	1973	1974	1975	1976	1977	1978
Preceding year=100	153.6	109.8	87.2	136.4	114.3	109.0	124.5	131.9
1970=100	153.6	168.7	147.1	200.6	229.3	249.9	311.2	329.7

Source: <u>Statisztikai Havi Közlemények</u>, 1978, no. 6, p. 54.

Table 8

Changes in the per Unit Cumulated Import Content of Exports
(1974 as % of 1972 values)

	Import content of earning	
	1 ruble	1 dollar
Import content from the ruble area	81.24	64.47
Import content from the dollar area	203.04	161.28

for dollars are used to manufacture exports for rubles. The relevant data are shown in Table 8. They also reveal a rising trend.

What conclusions can be drawn from the figures presented in Table 8? First, exports to both areas in general contain an ever greater percentage of imports and, in particular, a growing dollar import content. We also find that the direct and indirect nonruble import content of exports to the ruble area is roughly 20%, while the ruble content of exports to the dollar area is about 7%. A number of conclusions could be drawn from these figures, particularly for Hungary, in terms of export efficiency, export profitability, and sectoral development priorities. But we are not interested in these issues. Rather we are trying to ascertain whether this trend can continue, and how it should be evaluated.

These figures and others from the Central Statistical Office suggest that from 1970 until the end of the decade, the import content of production and consumption increased considerably in Hungary. The total import content of production increased from 20% to about 30%, that of consumption from 24 to 32%, and that of exports to about 25%. Some computations show that about one third of the imports from the ruble area are directly consumed (the comparable figure for imports from the dollar area being 18-25%), while the remainder is made up of primary and intermediate goods. The dollar import content is higher than the ruble import content in consumer goods and interme-

The Future of Socialist Economic Integration

diate goods, and dollar import intensity is increasing more rapidly. Trade transacted in convertible currencies among CMEA countries follows these patterns.

What do these trends suggest? Must we economize on imports in general? I believe not. The percentage of imported products in finished products and exports must certainly grow in the long run. Dynamic growth in exports of manufactures, especially of engineering products, can be achieved only if the industries increasingly specialize. We have already seen that this depends on a genuine division of production, not on the production of finished products. This inevitably suggests that production and exports will contain a growing percentage of imports. These trends are of common interest in the CMEA and are in complete agreement with our basic national interests as well. They mean that the engineering industry produces products with higher value added and exports them in growing amounts, and thus the increase in the per unit and the cumulated import content is exceeded by the increase in value. The same is true of light industry products. This holds to an even greater extent for the modern chemical industry, for the manufacturing base is now being built mainly by imports from nonruble countries.

The question is whether this necessary, positive process is promoted or impeded by our present internal accounting system. Considerable amounts of foreign exchange are handled in trade within the CMEA, and this would be all right if these currencies were equivalent. The fact that some of the raw materials used are imported, processed, and reexported is part of the process of the international division of labor. But today this trade takes place using foreign exchange accounts that are not equivalent. Due to differences in exchange rates and the usability of the transferable ruble, the purchasing power of the transferable ruble differs considerably from that of the nonruble currencies.

The direction of specialization and cooperation in particular sectors is significantly affected by daily economic policies and by the solution of day-to-day balance-of-payments problems.

Trade and Convertible Currencies

It seems obvious that if the tension in the balance of payments in nonruble currencies is growing, the nonruble content of exports to ruble areas must be diminished. This is the most obvious short-term conclusion for those in control of economic and trade policies. But this immobilizes structural change and hinders the development of modern industries. One solution is to obtain equivalent rates of exchange. Then this problem, which causes considerable tension in day-to-day economic policies, will disappear. We must recognize that as a result of growing East-West trade, only a single currency is possible — money that can be traded on the world market and is a measure of value and a means of circulation. The holder of this money can export to and import from domestic and foreign markets without discrimination, within a regulated framework.

Finally, let us assess the impact of direct and indirect trade on the Hungarian balance of payments. Data from the Central Statistical Office for 1976-78 showing total trade by groups of countries are presented in Table 9.

Table 10 shows how this trade is divided by groups of currencies.

From the data in Tables 9 and 10,[11] we can estimate indirect trade. According to the estimate used earlier, we assume that at current prices, about 20% of nonruble imports were used in exports to socialist countries, while about 10% of ruble imports were used in exports to the nonsocialist area. These items are just reexported by Hungary. Theoretically value is added in the course of processing a part imported from a capitalist country and exported to socialist countries. But because these items are reexported and do not represent Hungarian value added, they can be subtracted from trade data. For example, for 1977 data we can subtract 20% of hard currency imports — that is, 29 billion Ft — from the 143.8 billion Ft of imports as well as from the 120.2 billion Ft of exports to the ruble area. Conversely we deduct 10% of the imports from the ruble area — 12.3 billion Ft — from both the 123.5 billion Ft of ruble imports and the 118.4 billion Ft of exports to the nonruble area. Table 11 shows net figures for 1976-78.

The Future of Socialist Economic Integration

Table 9

Hungary's Trade 1976-78
(billion Ft)

	Socialist			Nonsocialist			Total		
	1976	1977	1978	1976	1977	1978	1976	1977	1978
Imports	124.0	140.8	155.7	106.0	126.5	145.2	230.1	267.3	300.9
Exports	124.0	147.9	146.7	80.9	90.7	94.0	204.9	238.6	240.7
Balance	.0	7.1	−9.0	−25.1	−35.8	−51.2	−25.2	−28.7	−60.2

Source: Central Statistical Office, Foreign Trade Statistical Yearbook, 1978, p. 12.

Table 10

Hungary's Trade in Currency Groups
(billion Ft)

	Ruble accounts			Nonruble accounts			Total		
	1976	1977	1978	1976	1977	1978	1976	1977	1978
Imports	108.8	123.5	136.3	121.2	143.8	164.7	230.1	267.3	300.9
Exports	101.3	120.2	120.9	103.6	118.4	119.8	204.9	238.6	240.7
Balance	−7.6	−3.4	−15.4	−17.6	−25.4	−44.9	−25.2	−28.7	−60.2

Table 11

Hungary's Net Balance of Trade
(billion Ft)

	Ruble accounts			Nonruble accounts			Total		
	1976	1977	1978	1976	1977	1978	1976	1977	1978
Imports	97.8	111.2	122.7	97.0	114.8	131.8	194.8	226.0	254.5
Exports	77.0	91.2	88.0	92.6	106.1	106.2	169.6	197.3	194.2
Balance	−20.8	−20.0	−34.7	−4.4	−8.7	−25.6	−25.4	−28.7	−60.3

Using these assumptions we can conclude that about two thirds of the total deficit of 28.7 billion Ft in 1977 came from ruble trade, and one third from nonruble trade. The reasons for this are complicated. The first point to note is the consequences of various developments in prices. In 1976, prices of imports from the West showed a significant rise and were followed rather slowly by socialist export prices. The terms of trade also deteriorated for many countries on the CMEA markets. Difficulty also arose in valuing goods at current prices due to differing prices and conversion ratios. Second, lacking an effective system of exchange rates that would realistically assure the equivalence of the ruble and the nonruble currencies, I have had to rely on Hungarian data only (and even this only by using expert's estimates).

c. Convertible Currencies in Accounting and
   Credit Transactions among CMEA Members

The use of convertible currencies has not been institutionalized in the current system of payments and accounting among the CMEA member countries. Although convertible currency settlements are thus external elements, they have existed in economic relations within the community from the outset, mainly for credits and some accounting transactions.

Credit operations can be bilateral or "central," meaning credit relations in convertible currencies with IBEC or the IIB. The convertible currencies appearing in these accounts may be either means of payment and account or special commodities.[12]

The volume of bilateral credit operations transacted in convertible currencies is not fully known, but the available data strongly suggest that it is important. (Due to timely extension of these credits during emergencies, they have often been of more importance than indicated by mere figures.) Such credits were granted mainly by the Soviet Union to other CMEA countries, including Hungary, until the early sixties. Bilateral credits raised and repaid in convertible currencies helped these countries solve some of their own domestic problems.

"Central" credits granted and repaid in convertible currencies are usually larger and have different goals than those of bilateral credit. This holds particularly for credits granted by the IBEC and the IIB. They are meant to be used for community tasks using funds raised partly in the member countries and partly on capitalist money markets.

The appearance of credits in convertible currency serving community purposes (and not merely solving one member country's problems) shows that the process of socialist cooperation and integration cannot dispense with convertible currencies. They have become part of the institutions of integration even if they are not part of the system of foreign trade settlements. Their special functions are that they make possible the flow of capital not directly related to the flow of trade within the community, and that through them additional joint investment on the community level can be achieved.[13]

A common feature of bilateral and to a certain extent "central" convertible currency credit operations is that these credits do not appear on the capitalist market as items that affect the creditworthiness of the country raising them; thus they improve these countries' relative position in this sense. But they do appear on the accounts of the country granting the credit if the latter refinances the credit granted on the capitalist money market.

If, in view of the above, we consider the role of credits and settlements granted and repaid in convertible foreign exchange within the community, we can conclude that:

— bilateral credits are mainly granted as aid and do not have a regular or institutional nature;

— "central" credits, however, have become an institutional part of socialist economic integration;

— in the case of refinancing, bilateral credits can reduce the credits of the member country to be raised from capitalists, while "central" credits more or less affect every member country's chances to raise credit for its own purposes. In some cases this makes the way "centrally" raised credits are allocated within the community very important;

— the purely financial (monetary) nature of such credit operations sharply differs from the nature of credit operations in transferable rubles, which are linked to the flow of commodities. Among other things, this lends greater flexibility to the former;

— a special subcase is credits granted in convertible currencies whose repayment is not made in the same currency but in transferable rubles, essentially in terms of commodities. In this case the convertible currency does not figure as a means of account and payment but as a special credited commodity.

In the case of such credits granted at a definite price (at the official rate of exchange of the transferable ruble), the money can be used to purchase other commodities whose price is also determined according to fixed principles.

The profitability of granting such credit depends, beyond interest rates, on the relative prices of the commodities that can be purchased and on the "hardness" of the latter. One element in price relations is the rate of exchange between the transferable ruble and the dollar.

In short, it appears that the capitalist foreign exchange is indispensable and has become an institutional element in the operations of socialist economic integration, as it has in the national economies.

This is shown, among other things, by IBEC operations transacted in transferable rubles in convertible currencies and by the relation between the two (see Table 12).

3. The Dialectics of Hard and Soft Commodities

The problem of hard and soft goods is an inevitable concomitant of the convertible currency and trade flows in internal CMEA trade. A number of studies have analyzed this problem. They rank commodities from hardest to softest as follows:
1) raw materials and fuels that can be sold on the world market;
2) modern equipment and parts;
3) standard engineering products that a country cannot obtain from its domestic production;
4) food and light industry products whose domestic supply fluctuates;
5) any products not mentioned above.

The Future of Socialist Economic Integration

Table 12

IBEC Transactions in Transferable Rubles and in
Convertible Currencies
(billions of transferable rubles)

Year	Mutual settlements		Transactions in convertible currencies		Ratio of transactions in convertible currencies to the volume of mutual settlements, %
	volume	annual growth in %	volume	annual growth in %	
1964	22.9	–	0.9	–	0.4
1965	24.1	105	2.0	222	8.3
1966	23.9	99	3.8	190	15.9
1967	26.6	111	9.0	237	33.8
1968	29.4	111	11.0	122	37.4
1969	32.1	109	13.7	125	42.7
1970	35.4	110	21.2	155	59.9
1971	39.3	111	23.6	111	60.1
1972	43.3	110	27.2	115	62.8
1973	47.4	109	35.8	132	75.5
1974	52.6	111	58.2	163	110.6
1975	66.9	127	63.1	108	94.3
1976	82.5	123	70.0	111	84.8
1977	94.7	115	79.2	113	83.6

Source: IBEC bulletins for 1976 and 1977.

The IBEC bulletin does not give the components of the transactions in convertible currencies. Presumably they include settlements of some transactions in East-West trade, deposits and credits of Western banks, accounts of other international organizations, e.g., of the IIB, as well as the capital and convertible currency reserves of the IBEC.

The range of these products changes from time to time (partly every year). The categorization fundamentally affects the structure of mutual trade. This is shown by the figures for 1977 in Table 13.

The signs of attempts to achieve balanced trade in each group of commodities are so obvious that no special comment is needed. It is also clear that hardness and softness affect the structure, accounting, mutual trade policies, prices, efficiency, and internal flow of convertible currencies. Let us examine them.

Table 13

Pattern of Commodity Trade among Hungary and Five CMEA Countries in 1977
(percentage distribution)

	Bulgaria		CSSR		Poland		GDR		Romania	
	exports	imports	exports	imports	exports	imports	exports	imports	exports	imports
Machines	57.0	54.5	43.4	47.2	41.5	44.0	56.1	63.6	45.8	44.5
Fuels, mineral products	12.2	12.3	6.2	19.4	16.7	22.5	5.5	6.1	21.9	16.3
Chemicals fertilizers	5.3	8.7	2.9	8.0	8.0	3.5	0.9	11.5	11.8	12.6
Building materials	0.9	1.3	4.5	3.4	1.0	10.8	0.9	1.6	2.0	6.0
Other industrial materials	4.3	0.8	2.7	4.2	4.1	2.4	2.2	2.3	1.4	1.9
Agricultural products	5.0	6.4	11.6	0.3	3.0	1.8	6.7	0.0	7.6	6.8
Food	0.7	7.2	14.2	3.4	10.2	4.5	16.2	1.2	2.2	3.6
Industrial consumer goods	14.6	8.8	14.5	14.1	15.5	10.5	11.5	13.7	7.3	8.3

Total = 100.0

Source: Central Statistical Office, Külkereskedelmi Statistikai Évkönyv, 1977.

The Future of Socialist Economic Integration

Trade underlying settlements in transferable rubles is based on five-year and annual bilateral trade agreements specified in physical units. This mode of planning trade fully corresponds to the requirements of directive planning. Within the trade agreement, linking exports and imports of certain groups of commodities proved to be the best way to secure markets for export items that are not strongly competitive and to secure imports that, given the export conditions, seem most advantageous. In this sense the specification of trade agreements in physical units and the strictly bilateral balancing of trade also have important repercussions on trade policy, the more so the more problematic it would be for some country without such agreement to acquire economically necessary exports with the smallest amount and best structure of imports possible. Of course, the volume and composition of bilateral trade are influenced by other factors as well.

Obviously, in the system presented above, trade deficits with one country cannot, in general, be balanced by a claim against a third country. The creditor country cannot assume that it can secure from the third country the imports actually needed; in the current system this could only happen in exceptional cases.

Hardening of the export pattern, improved commodity salability, and increasing flexibility of trade could lead directly to the transferability of the internal accounting currency. It seems that the "most natural" path leading from the present system to multilateralism is the "hardening" of commodity trade. It is a process of key importance not only for the possibility of currency transferability but also for the general development of industry in the community. The prime mover of this process is the rise in demands made on imports, behind which we find a general rise in the need for efficiency in the national economies. Importers harden the commodity pattern of trade partly by spurring competition from imports from capitalist countries and partly by duplicating production lines in the member countries.

This change in the pattern of trade is, of course, also aided by the changes in export contracts initiated by exporters who are trying to improve supply. Obviously the purpose of such initiatives is to improve the export position of the country and its terms of trade.

Specialization, because it can also enhance the salability of commodities exported within the community, also can promote "harder" trade and, through harder trade, a more convertible transferable ruble. But if the technical standards of the products produced in the framework of specialization are not high enough, perhaps because markets are felt to be safe, no such effect will be felt.

Thus the hardening of the commodity pattern of exports of CMEA member countries, particularly with respect to manufactured products, is underway and continues to be the "natural" condition for developing the transferable ruble. However, expectations about the rate of this process are important. The transformation of the composition of exports always involves costs and, frequently, risks. Exporting countries have only a certain amount of funds for this purpose, and they are willing to use all these funds only if they are forced to do so by importers' demands, or if risk is not too great. Trends in foreign trade prices also affect this process.

The categories of "hardness" and "softness" are affected not only by prices but also by differences in views regarding the proper interpretation of efficiency. We know from the international economic literature that some economists in the CMEA countries now believe manufacturing to be efficient and the production of raw materials to be inefficient. This view should be examined in terms of prices.

We should begin with the fact that our contract prices, although based on world market prices, also reflect bilateral bargaining to secure balanced trade (balanced in terms of physical units) in which world market prices determine the direction of price changes but not their magnitude. It follows that price does not reflect the scarcity of the goods. There is no correlation between hardness and softness and price, for the imbalance between demand and supply would be reflected in prices, not in hardness and its effect on the rigidity of the commodity pattern. (The interrelations between price and hardness are discussed in detail elsewhere.)[14]

In spite of this the hardness of commodities is a real economic factor; it is reflected in balanced trade by commodity group. The fact that balanced trade by commodity group is more important than price reflects the results of bargaining and linkage in physical terms. This has repercussions on efficiency calculations. Hungary, for example, cannot transform profits deriving from higher prices of its machinery exports, which are considered "soft" but at the same time efficient, into "hard" raw material imports in bilateral trade (considered inefficient according to current economic concepts) because the structural proportions are predetermined. Therefore, because of the nature of the linkage, a country cannot use larger receipts due to high prices to purchase the commodities it needs but must settle for those its partner has linked to raw materials exports and in the amounts its partner wants to sell.

In terms of a price system, this suggests that the soft articles obtained in exchange for higher prices or "comparative advantages" are either not always needed or, if needed, are required to a much lesser extent than reflected by prices. Thus the price of a soft import good is too high; the buyer pays more than the good is worth to him. Yet the CMEA countries benefit by the exchange because in this system they can sell articles they could not sell on the world market, at least not at the same price.

This system makes it necessary to calculate the gains from trade subjectively. Subjective estimation or clever bargaining determines how scarcities can develop and be settled in bilateral trade given the nontransferability of claims. Noneconomic considerations also play a role. Trade is determined by linkage, and scarcity is reflected only through the give-and-take of bargaining. Under bilateralism trade is conducted by determining how many units of some hard article are equal to so many units of another hard article. And trade in soft commodities must also balance.

Trade and Convertible Currencies

This is why this system produces a completely topsy-turvy logic. Although iron ore, coke, crude oil, soft sawnwood, etc., are considered hard commodities, they are also viewed by planners as economically unprofitable to produce. On the other hand, while conveyor belts, agricultural machinery, and other machines are deemed soft goods in the CMEA, they are considered profitable to produce by each country.[15] Furthermore parts imported for convertible currency are hard articles, but once they are processed and installed in machines, they become soft machinery products.

Finally, we must determine how hardness and softness are related to the development of internal trade accounted in convertible foreign exchange. If a member country feels that the exports from a partner country have become too soft — that is, increasingly it cannot satisfy the demands of the former — an opportunity arises to further CMEA trade. In this case further softening can be forestalled if the first country is willing to increase its exports of hard commodities only for convertible foreign exchange if it cannot import commodities of adequate hardness. Such steps can be expected first on the part of those countries that have not made satisfactory progress in the production and export of up-to-date articles. In such cases the ratio of settlements in convertible foreign exchange would rise.

Owing to changes in product patterns and relative scarcities, those goods considered hard may change over the course of years. Despite this caveat, using the structure of Hungary's trade within the CMEA and statistics on trade of about 600 commodities, I calculate that in the midseventies hard goods made up roughly 60-70% of Hungary's exports and 70-75% of its imports. The remainder was soft. All the evidence indicates that soft goods are generally machinery. The main problem thus lies not in settlements and trade but in production. The task is to achieve so radical a transformation of the present production structure that at least half of all engineering products become competitive commodities salable on any market.

Experience shows that potential developments of the CMEA countries' economic relations among their own members and with the West have a mutual impact. As indicated above, these developments are moving in two directions. Increased productivity and efficiency of economic relations within the community are hindered if significant tensions arise in economic relations with the West, while these tensions can be overcome most reliably by successful development of community relations. It has also become obvious that a forced restriction of economic relations with the capitalist countries and autarkic tendencies lead to deterioration in efficiency and in the quality of development in the majority of CMEA countries, just as would neglect of relations within the community.

These facts mean that convertible currencies and capitalist money markets must be considered more consciously among the factors influencing member countries' community relations. Since this question will continue to occupy an important place in the domestic economic problems of the member countries, especially the smaller ones, the countries will be able to work even more intensively on extending integration if this factor is emphasized in community economic policy in a way that promotes economic integration. Lacking an appropriate policy on convertible currencies, proposals for integration will be neither realistic nor practicable.

The deterioration in the terms of trade that has occurred for the smaller CMEA countries since the midseventies and the enormous increase in recent years in the community's need for convertible foreign exchange have led to large hard currency debts and balance-of-payments deficits among member countries. This has occurred as business conditions in the capitalist world have become more difficult and, in some cases, as capitalist credit has been tightened. The member countries (like many other countries on a similar level of development) were also unprepared for the increased demands of exporting to the West, including choices on product development and flexibility in marketing. However, a growing indirect trade in convertible currency has emerged within the CMEA which, in contrast to direct trade, is a natural part of technological development.

Trade and Convertible Currencies

Because of this, adjusting the member countries' convertible currencies balance of payments has become an urgent task. However, our question is whether expansion of the community's convertible currency trade at the expense of trade in transferable rubles can be of assistance in this process.

First, it should be pointed out that if the situation remains the same, present trade conducted in convertible currency will neither cease nor increase substantially. However, indirect trade will rise. Second, while transferable ruble trade will decline further in the member countries' total foreign trade because of the need to increase exports to the West, this in itself does not entail an end to increases in transferable ruble trade nor an absolute decline in this trade.

Intra-CMEA trade in hard currencies also affects the future of the transferable ruble system. From this point of view, whether the members succeed in making the transferable ruble truly multilateral is a question of secondary importance, for even if they succeed, the transferable ruble will continue to be a closed system just as difficult for outside partners to enter as clearing systems in general. It will still not be convertible with Western currencies, and it will hinder the CMEA countries from participating in the world economy with increasing flexibility and weight using their own financial instruments.

If the joint monetary institutions are maintained, the transferable ruble — in the long run — must become "convertible"; that is, a new, convertible CMEA currency must be developed. This currency will have to be genuinely convertible. Clearing accounts will then have to be replaced by a system of convertible currencies. Thus, if over the long run the socialist countries want to assume a role in the world economy in keeping with their influence in world politics, and if they want to make use of their national currency or common foreign exchange, ultimately they will have to move to a form of convertibility.

The decisive changes of the seventies make this development urgent. On the one hand this period has seen the emergence of a new economic order. On the other hand there have been fundamental changes in the positions of the participants and their major alliances in the world economy. There has been a decisive change in East-West cooperation and trade and the import of technology. There has been a great increase in the volume of know-how and technology imported from the West and an expansion in cooperation and specialization projects.

Economic growth in the socialist countries has entered the stage of transition from extensive to intensive growth, largely independently of changes in relations. This is clearly a positive development. But at the same time, it also shows that it is becoming necessary to restructure and reorganize all the factors and forces affecting economic growth, including foreign trade and settlements. In addition this must be done in a considerably more difficult and complex world economic environment than existed a decade ago.

The transition from extensive to intensive growth has had a novel influence on trade and accounting. The slogans of higher efficiency and improved quality have generally been adopted in our countries. It follows that users have caused a considerable increase in demands on the products traded. The users' demand that top-quality, highly efficient products be supplied is perfectly rational and logical. However, the conditions for exporters to meet this demand have been created slowly and with greater difficulty. Thus a contradiction exists between the increasing, justified demands by consumers and the standards of the product mix offered by exporters. Financially it is reflected in the growing proportion of direct and indirect trade in convertible currencies and in the differences in domestic and foreign trade pricing.

While the problems I have mentioned appear superficially to be related to monetary and financial relations, their origin is not solely financial in nature. In reality we are facing the effects of the present socialist international economic system in the area of foreign exchange. And while changing planning methods and coordinating plans can increase efficiency, these changes also have high costs. A study of the proposals for a change in the system controlling trade and related monetary problems indicates that change would be an extremely lengthy process. However, while in the sixties the demands for change were formulated primarily in terms of theory, practical developments are now a much more important force. Some solution must be found for the problems outlined here, either through a greater role for the national currencies or convertibility of the transferable ruble. The solution could assume two forms: either the differing price systems could be brought closer together through internal financial means, premiums, and discounts, or we must seek new paths. However, the search for new paths, including the convertibility of national currencies or the increased role of the collective currency, is not enough. It is not sufficient to reform the monetary system alone.

In the final analysis we need to establish conditions for regulated socialist competition. Monetary questions and changes in marketing also affect economic policy, particularly regarding the contradiction between the established industrial structure, the steadily growing demands of users, and the production of inefficient, uncompetitive goods.

This contradiction affects employment and other internal factors. However, there are also external factors. Like our own monetary system, the international monetary system is struggling with many difficulties and is still far from perfect. Crises beyond those now apparent are also coming. The neglect of stability and the present international monetary system, based on the dollar as the key currency and reflecting the interests of the industrially most advanced countries, are not suitable for the development of an international monetary system embracing the whole world.

An obstacle to bringing the two financial systems closer together and solving these problems is that while markets and prices play an important role in relations among the capitalist countries, they remain in the background in the case of the CMEA countries. Our domestic problems close the path to perfecting the monetary mechanism of socialist integration. It is becoming clear that we can advance only by introducing a better, efficiency-oriented system of economic control and management that encourages and rewards the ability to meet international competition; it must be introduced as a consistent system of instruments and institutions. Of course, we must also place the defensive instruments of our present financial system — strict quotas and bilateralism — on a new basis. Furthermore, because events have come to a head, this must be done soon.

Finally, international monetary cooperation must promote the establishment of a new, rational international division of labor. However, this can only happen if the countries of the world treat each other as equals. The level of economic development of the individual countries and the special circumstances arising from their social and economic systems must be taken into account. The economic system of the socialist countries, based on social ownership of the means of production and national economic planning, must be one of the decisive elements in the establishment of a world monetary system.

Chapter IX
Efficiency and the Problem of Its Measurement in Production Integration

1. Introduction

In the past we have achieved important results in the study of certain complex methodological problems of the international socialist division of labor. However, we still lag on the question of efficiency. At international scholarly gatherings it is still quite correctly claimed that we do not have criteria for evaluating efficiency on the level of the CMEA. There is no consensus on the criteria that would unequivocally tell whether a given proposal for the socialist international division of labor is efficient. Thus a number of different methodologies are used to determine the efficiency of proposals for production cooperation. Arbitrary evaluation of the objectives of socialist economic integration and the variety of systems and criteria for calculating the efficiency of economic cooperation lead to subjective selection of forms and directions of cooperation. This might ultimately become a major obstacle to developing integration processes.

2. Efficiency in CMEA Production Integration

If we take the CMEA as a whole as our starting point, standards of efficiency will differ from those used by the separate countries. Moreover efficient use and development of the resources of the CMEA region could be achieved more successfully by considering the region as a whole and adopting a uniform development policy, rather than taking the interests of the national economies as the starting point. However, since we now use the one-sided concept of production integration, such an approach can only be adopted later, when both market and production integration are applied. Thus efforts to establish such a policy would be unrealistic at present and probably will remain so for a long time to come.

We must therefore assume that the national economies of the CMEA countries will continue to operate and develop separately for the foreseeable future.

The argument above clearly points to the conclusion that in studying the economic development of the CMEA region and the efficiency of development, we must take the individual national economies as our starting point. Therefore efficient economic development of the individual countries must be the criterion for efficiency of economic development within the CMEA.

However, global considerations, based on natural and other conditions, could come to the fore when formulating long-term CMEA development plans, predictions, and policy measures, particularly with respect to sectoral development and target programs. In such cases the decisive link must be selected, and the capacities of the individual countries and limitations on the flow of production factors must be taken into consideration. In short, we must consider the limited possibilities that are available in this stage of production integration.

We must also take another circumstance into consideration in the study of efficiency on the CMEA level, namely, the differing levels of development of the CMEA countries. Higher forms of cooperation can be attained only among industrialized countries on a relatively similar level of development. It is thus in the common interest to narrow the differences in the levels of development. Moreover, it cannot be in the interest of any socialist country to gain unwarranted economic advantage over another socialist country in the course of economic development.

On this basis we can consider the economic development of the CMEA region efficient and successful if cooperation by the member countries makes the maximum contribution to increasing the efficiency of development in the individual countries, and if, within the framework of production integration, we can achieve optimal use of the resources of the CMEA region, increasingly balanced development, and a trend toward eliminating differences in economic development among the member countries. We must determine whether proposals for cooperation embody these goals.

Therefore we cannot approach the question of overall CMEA efficiency by taking into account only national efficiency requirements, nor can we approach it through the present CMEA efficiency standards. The theoretical approach to efficiency leads through the combined determination of national and CMEA optima.[1]

Limited models can be formulated that are aimed at developing an optimal division of labor and that originate from a national optimum. These models need to be constructed because the individual countries' plans for optimum foreign trade would be in vain if their plans did not accord with the ideas and economic potentials of their partners.

Practical application of these models still lies in the future, and in their present state these models are not free from problems. András Simon believes that the initial steps toward practical application are:

— knowing the production possibilities of the individual countries by sectors;

— finding possible trade-offs of objectives and resources between the national models;

— constructing an international model based on these trade-offs. The greatest difficulty lies in establishing the rates of substitution of the different products and determining the extent of substitutability.

Although this method is not applicable under present condiditions, in the not too distant future, computations of this type will serve as a theoretical basis for economic cooperation among the socialist countries. In the distant future plans for international socialist division of labor can also presumably be drawn up using this approach.

3. Minimization of Costs or Maximization of Profits

Up to now I have tried to shed light on the interpretation of efficiency. Next I would like to examine a few concrete problems. The first concerns the maximization of profits or minimization of costs.

Looking at the question from the theoretical point of view, there is general agreement that the socialist international division of labor develops most successfully in those sectors and industries in which production is most profitable. The lack of such profits unavoidably leads to the development of duplicate lines of production, which is often inefficient in terms of technological development and quality and the common interests of the CMEA countries.

Mutual advantage is one of the most important factors affecting production integration. Some people hold that mutual advantage can be secured in specialization and cooperation only if the efficiency of the integration measures and prices in foreign trade are based on the minimum costs of production.

To better understand this problem, let me recall the methodological mistakes and deficiencies made by the CMEA Economic Standing Committee in elaborating efficient plans for the international socialist division of labor in the late fifties and early sixties. At that time they compared domestic production costs of the individual products, using some common denominator to find a plan assuring minimal investment costs and inputs. Practically this meant that if some product could be produced in several countries, that country should be preferred in which the product could be produced with minimum inputs. A logical consequence of the application of the principle of minimum costs is the clause attached on such occasions, namely, that the profits from the production be distributed among the countries affected. The following passage displays this principle:

> The aim of mutual division of labor among the socialist countries participating in cooperation is not to attain additional surplus product. The aim is for the country to satisfy its needs for some product at lower costs than would be possible if the product were produced at home. The socialist international division of labor will become economical and will contribute to the raising of the productivity of social labor in every member country only in this case. Therefore, in selecting directions for production cooperation, the starting point is a country's need for the products and precise knowledge about possible ways to meet these needs most efficiently.[2]

Yet aside from the methodological difficulties in calculating and comparing costs, it is not mere coincidence that the principle of minimum costs has not solved the problems of efficiency in the international socialist division of labor to this very day. We can see that with regard to price and the problem of division of economic gains, we are still where we were ten years ago.

What are the defects in adopting the principle of minimum costs?

First, we know that the socialist countries are on different economic and technological levels of development. When evaluating international specialization plans, it is usually most rational in terms of present efficiency to develop specialization in the relatively most developed countries. Obviously the less developed countries are not very interested in such cooperation; but the more advanced countries are also not interested, for they would have to decide the price at which to trade the specialized products and a method to divide the economic gains from specialization among the countries.

I agree with the Soviet economist I. Motorin, who writes in this context:

> This method is fundamentally wrong, since it sets out from a thesis that can be applied in a single country but not in a community of nations, and it cannot be used in every case even in a single country. Thus the problem of developing new products cannot be solved according to the principle of minimum costs, particularly when new economic regions have to be developed.[3]

Specialization brings a number of quantifiable and nonquantifiable advantages to both the producer and the buyer. If, therefore, the principle of specialization suggests that production should be located where costs would be minimized, and that the resultant profits must be divided between the producer and the seller, this will lead to autarky, or at least a decline in intra-CMEA trade; for if the producer can sell on a different market at the same or a higher price, and he need not share his profit with anyone, he will naturally go where he can get a higher price and higher profit. But this is only one aspect of the matter. The other is that if we minimize costs and require division of profits derived from increased efficiency, then cost reduction itself will become irrational, i.e., there will be no motive to continuously adjust production to the productivity and quality standards of the advanced industrial countries, particularly if this involves additional investment.

What conclusion should be drawn from all this? Let us turn again to Motorin, who writes:

> All this shows that at the present stage of socialist economic integration there cannot be uniform norms and criteria for the socialist international division of labor that would hold for all countries in the community. Every socialist country, as the only and indivisible owner of its means of production, establishes its own criteria and norms of efficiency. Under present conditions mutual advantages can be secured only if the proposed variants of production cooperation are implemented by each country itself, and if each performs efficiency computations

Efficiency and Its Measurement

according to its own norms and criteria. If any variant is efficient for a given country, it is efficient for the community as a whole; conversely the variant that does not suit the individual countries also cannot be accepted as optimal for the whole.[4]

I fully agree with these remarks. I have reached a similar conclusion through analysis of possible national and CMEA optima. But this position can only be accepted with a reservation, namely, that national efficiency calculations must be used where cooperation is being achieved without unity of production and market integration, and where the division of labor is being achieved while forcing trade and monetary relations into the background. However, this is only one side of the matter. The other is actually much more important.

If each country actually determines its own norms and criteria for efficiency, it follows that it decides on participation in specialization and cooperation on the basis of its own national system of values. If this is so, then under the present concept of production integration, if a specialization project is profitable for a given country, it is profitable for the whole community, and vice versa: if it is not in the interests of individual countries, then it cannot be accepted as optimal for the whole.

In my opinion this is the key question in understanding the whole current concept of production integration. It suggests the following. This principle and concept are valid only when autonomous, independent, sovereign national economies take part in the integration of production, and when the free flow of production factors among the countries does not exist. Basically this is the essence of autarkic development. If the essence of economic integration is the merger of national markets and enforcement of the requirements for CMEA-level optima and efficiency, ensuring the free flow of investment among the countries is an indispensable condition. However, investments must flow to that area in which they are most efficient because otherwise there is no point in freeing investment flows. (Naturally, the development of backward regions requires priority treatment.

But we have not yet faced the issue of regional development within the CMEA.) What we therefore need to know is what CMEA-level efficiency is on the basis of a given criterion, so that we can use it to evaluate the inputs of the different countries. In this case we no longer begin with the assumption that what is efficient for one country is also efficient for the community, but we assume that what is profitable on the world market is also efficient for the community. And this enormous difference is the heart of the whole question.

Take the case of electronic pocket calculators. Recall that we imported electronic pocket calculators from Bulgaria for 100 rubles each. Then we began to manufacture them ourselves, but the imported parts alone cost $15, to say nothing of domestic inputs. The Hungarian foreign trade enterprise then imported finished electronic pocket calculators from Hong Kong for $15, and we stopped imports from Bulgaria.

The essence of the matter is obvious here. If we establish our efficiency criteria on the basis of the world market, we can immediately set topsy-turvy matters straight. It is quite clear that in this example it was profitable for Bulgaria to produce electronic pocket calculators for a price of 100 rubles, and from Bulgaria's point of view this was efficient. But it is also clear that it was not efficient for the community; indeed, the Bulgarian product simply could not be imported into Hungary because it was not competitive on the world market at that price. Thus the core of the matter is: if we want to make progress in specialization and cooperation in terms of efficiency, it is crucial to find a uniform criterion by which to evaluate individual domestic inputs, a criterion with which both the producer and the buyer can be satisfied. If we are to make progress in economic integration, it is indispensable to evaluate labor inputs identically within the CMEA. It is thus indispensable that work be evaluated in the same way in Bulgaria as in Hungary and in the same way in Hungary as in Czechoslovakia. And this uniform standard can only be set by the judgment of the world market.

In discussing efficiency in terms of minimum costs or maximum profits, we find that we are in a theoretical blind alley. The problem arises from the fact that when market and money relations are forced into the background, and an autarkic concept of the development of production and isolation from outside economic influences predominate, efficiency can only be achieved to a limited extent.

The only way I can see out of this theoretical blind alley is to achieve unity of production and market integration. We must implement a concept that allows us to apply efficiency criteria and make economic decisions for national development in keeping with world market requirements in order to develop efficiency at the CMEA level. In this way we can ensure increasingly efficient production on an ever higher quality level in all sectors of CMEA economic life by making full use of the economic advantages of the socialist system. When efficiency criteria and decisions based on national interests increasingly give way to economic decisions corresponding to the CMEA optima and international interests, production will reach world market efficiency levels and may even exceed them.

4. Conclusions

1. Within a given national economy the basic objective of investments is maximization of efficiency, but this condition must be supplemented with other sets of conditions that link technological development to the world market. Thus the highest aim of the socialist international division of labor is to raise the national and international efficiency of social production, and the most general indicator for this is the growth of per capita net national income in the individual countries. Therefore in economic development the most important thing is to decide through what factors we can obtain the most rapid growth in per capita net income. For a smaller or medium-sized country, the highest level of labor productivity and the highest level of profitability can be obtained by joining in the worldwide international division of labor in the most advantageous way.

The Future of Socialist Economic Integration

Thus, in general, plans for economic development that allow the most advantageous increase in the national income of the country in the framework of the socialist and the worldwide international division of labor can be considered optimal. This optimization is realistic only if it is carried out in the individual CMEA member countries separately and in a coordinated way.

2. The next important lesson is that we should differentiate between small and large countries when examining problems of CMEA-level efficiency. The greater the area of a country, its density of population, and its natural resources, and the more developed its forces of production, the more comprehensive the development of its economy can be. In such countries the sectors of production mutually complement each other and can develop proportionally to each other, for the domestic market is adequately large. If, however, a country is small and poor in natural resources, it must fit into the international division of labor by developing those areas in which it has a comparative advantage. This aspect is generally completely neglected in theoretical studies and in the economic literature of the CMEA. As a matter of fact, if we examine only the Hungarian experience and compare efficiency criteria from the viewpoints of a small and a large country, we find that in determining the efficiency of the economic development plans of a small country, several very important criteria are missing. For example, there is no mention of the strategic importance of developing particular products or production sectors. In a big country, however, the production of an otherwise uneconomical product can be started because of strategic and other considerations. The efficiency requirements of a small country are determined much more by the need to rapidly adapt to the world market than by overall efficiency requirements.

3. In medium-sized and small countries foreign trade plays a major role in changes in utilization of materials and in production. In Hungary, for example, the increases in the percentage of materials imported in production are similar to those of the capitalist countries that are most dependent on raw material imports. The growth of imports is a particular cause for

concern because there is a close relationship in our country between production and the growth of imports of raw materials. Increased production was based to an inordinate extent on imported materials, particularly primary materials. The share of imported materials is particularly high in the metallurgy, chemicals, and light industries. The total import content of 100 Ft of final products in 1975 was almost 54 Ft in metallurgy, about 55 Ft in the chemical industry, and 40 Ft in light industry.[5]

The greater the exports of a country, and the greater the number of relatively profitable exports, the greater can be the volume of its imports and the number of unprofitable products whose domestic production can be reduced or eliminated. Conversely, the smaller the profitably produced exports of a country, the greater the extent to which it is compelled to continue to produce unprofitable products domestically. Thus foreign trade is an organic ingredient in shaping the structure of the economy.

Changes in trade patterns are basically determined by structural changes in the national economy. The volume and pattern of trade develop in accordance with the development and structure of the economy. But the higher the proportion of foreign trade relative to national income, the more foreign trade influences changes in the internal structure of the economy. The efficiency of national production and the profitability of foreign trade increasingly depend on each other. Thus in the concept of production integration, efficiency requirements are determined for the smaller countries more and more by the constraints of foreign trade. But our national prices and our national system of valuation are in themselves insufficient for determining which products can be profitably exported. The judgment of the world market needs to be directly taken into account.

4. Finally, efficiency computations should also be related to the system of domestic economic control. They must be made starting from the recognition that no economic system is good everywhere and at all times. The more economic policy plans influence individual decisions, the more deliberate the transformation of the economic structure can be. Ultimately the

highest criterion for the quality of the economic structure is efficiency. An economic structure can be said to be efficient if it permits the optimal allocation of economic resources in harmony with social policy objectives. Thus an efficient economy is one in which, while social requirements are met, optimal growth of national income continues. For national income to constantly and steadily rise, the economic structure must change. Today such change can rest on the results of technological progress and on the advantages inherent in the worldwide international division of labor.

Favorably influencing change is a long-term and constant task for the economic mechanism. The most important goal is to promote through international specialization and cooperation rapid and large-scale development of particular "carrier" products, particularly in those branches of manufacturing in which the application of modern technologies has a strong tradition. We must determine whether there are developments in the individual mechanisms that lead to economic inefficiencies. The key to this lies in the enterprises. They find out most rapidly if some of their products are unprofitable, and the correction of this problem depends primarily on their expertise. Analysis of profits must be supported by analysis of prices and of production costs. In enterprise decisions profit is an important but insufficient criterion, since investment decisions are aimed at the future, and profit changes over time. It is therefore important for import competition to force enterprises to modernize their products.

Chapter X
The Influence of East-West Cooperation on CMEA Production Integration

1. The Influence of the New World Economic Order on Production Integration

CMEA production integration is not a closed process. It is influenced by East-West economic cooperation, whose continued development bears witness to a sense of reality on the part of the Western countries. In the future we can assume that in addition to the individual trade deals, ultimately forms of longer-lasting cooperation — financial agreements, compensation deals, license agreements, and gradually, industrial cooperation projects — will come to the fore. They will have a strong influence on the economic growth of the CMEA countries.

Since the early seventies two major processes in East-West economic relations have been influencing and will continue to influence production integration: the development of credit relations and the external economic strategy of the USSR.

The major investment programs of the CMEA countries have involved the need for large-scale credits and will continue to do so. The outlines of the new credit policy now taking shape and the trends on the European money and capital markets lead us to the conclusion that — at least until the mideighties — credit relations will become of ever increasing importance not only in covering the import needs of the socialist countries and consolidating their balances of payments but also in determining the more important economic development projects. Moreover the intensive nature of trade in machinery and technology, accompanied by large-scale credit deals, unlike the previous simple deals, creates a certain stability and continuity and closer technical relations.

However, this increased debt from the West has lead to major problems, especially for the smaller CMEA countries. The extent of indebtedness and the demand for credit are now being harmonized with the judgment of the market. As credit conditions harden, the CMEA countries may increasingly emphasize establishing conditions for a coordinated credit-raising policy. This in turn raises the problem of the institutional background of credit relations. A capitalist credit supply exists and is growing, and the costs of raising credit are also rising. Obviously, extended relations suggest an increase in long-term credits. Furthermore competition among the advanced capitalist countries on the CMEA market may result in a gradual improvement of conditions favorable to us. These conditions may take the form of a lower rate of interest in order to ensure stable markets. The smaller CMEA countries must therefore take advantage of this opportunity.

Growing indebtedness also means that it is in the interest of both Eastern and Western partners to increase the solvency of the CMEA countries. Solvency can be increased in two ways. On the one hand the Western countries should considerably prolong the repayment period of credits and extend more favorable interest rates for industrial cooperation agreements. On the other hand the smaller CMEA countries must make a radical change in their production and export structure in the interest of increasing their Western exports, including integration of production. In order to increase their abilities to earn foreign exchange and service their debts, they must develop industrial sectors that ensure major new opportunities for sales on the world market.[1] They must therefore increase the integration of production, turn out industrial products of good quality, and improve related services. Several joint ventures are also needed in this connection. Although the volume of credit can be expected to drop, relations will become more complex.

The problem of the balance of trade and debts of the CMEA countries is partly a consequence of the present economic downturn in the Western countries; but as the Western economy strengthens, it will help these countries improve their production relations. Therefore, although the socialist countries may introduce import restrictions in the consumer sector, they cannot slow down their economic development too drastically because this will hinder the implementation of their long-term plans. They must therefore continue to rely on Western financial sources and must provide for radical changes in their economic and export structures.

The new developments can thus play a positive role, on the one hand, in the improvement of East-West economic relations and, on the other, in the development of CMEA production integration. The main manifestations of this are strengthening the elements of stability, strengthening the long-term approach on both sides, strengthening elements of cooperation in mutual production integration, and eliminating duplicate projects as much as possible.

The other basic influence on CMEA production integration is exercised by Soviet-Western trade and changes in the Soviet Union's external economic strategy.

In recent years there has been a change in Soviet commercial policy toward satisfying demands created by development projects through trade with the advanced capitalist countries. This line will continue because the Soviet economy will continue to grow and become increasingly complex in the coming years, and the main directions of its development are shaped by the new, modern sectors of its industry. It is becoming increasingly difficult to separate the development of individual sectors of industry from a steady rise in the technological level and efficiency of the whole economy. Consumer needs are also imposing growing demands on increasing productivity. Therefore it is increasingly recognized in the Soviet Union that the international division of labor must be taken into account not only in targeted areas or in resolving temporary gaps in development in various areas but also in serving as a starting point for determining the basic directions for development of the national economy.

The Soviet Union's increased participation in the international division of labor will cause the development of new forms of foreign economic relations. They will primarily appear in the further development of the present process, in which simple foreign trade deals increasingly give way to the establishment of lasting technological, production, and trade relations. Thus we can expect intergovernmental agreements and long-term credit relations, the development of scientific and technical cooperation, and different forms of investment and production cooperation.

It can be seen that the Soviet Union will continue to buy mainly capital goods from the developed capitalist countries. In addition food imports will continue, while raw materials will continue to constitute the bulk of exports, since the most important development plans and cooperation agreements provide for an increase in raw material exports. Another continuing trend is that the energy crisis in the capitalist world will influence Soviet foreign trade in several ways. In the first place, it will improve the terms of trade, which will strengthen the Soviet Union's payments position and will facilitate continuation of the policy of large-scale purchases. It will also create better conditions for raising credits by substantially increasing the Soviet Union's debt-servicing ability. However, imports will continue to be selectively determined.

The Soviet Union will transact the greater part of its foreign trade in the coming years with the CMEA countries. While further dynamic growth in trade with the advanced capitalist countries could result in a further reduction in the CMEA countries' share in total Soviet foreign trade, this will not slow down the growth rate of trade between the Soviet Union and the other CMEA countries. It is important that the structural composition of trade within the CMEA improve so that growth continues. In certain areas, because of growing Soviet demands for quality, the CMEA countries will encounter more difficulties than in the past in exporting manufactured articles to the Soviet Union.

The Soviet market is setting stiffer conditions for the CMEA countries, necessitating a major increase in competitiveness and a substantial improvement in efficiency and quality.[2]

At the same time, a shift in Soviet imports of capital goods from the advanced capitalist countries could create new opportunities for cooperation within the CMEA, for example, in the heavy engineering industry. The possible extent of specialization and the advantages resulting for the other countries must definitely be taken into consideration. Moreover, the Soviet market is enormous and cannot be saturated, even in part, with Western industrial products.

In short, production integration is being greatly influenced by growing East-West economic relations and world market price changes. On the basis of the needs of internal socioeconomic development, a long-term Soviet foreign economic policy has taken shape that takes into account the international division of labor as a lasting and constant factor in determining the directions and modes of economic development. Improvement in technological standards and efficiency as a result of such a long-term policy could be one of the decisive factors in raising cooperation within the CMEA to a higher level, particularly in terms of technological factors. At the same time, as the expansion of the Soviet Union's Western economic relations and international détente emerge as constant factors, these developments could create favorable opportunities for the other, smaller CMEA countries to participate more actively in the East-West division of labor and to better exploit their potential. This process could be hampered by inadequate growth in export capabilities and problems with indebtedness, and from the political angle by swings in détente and increased tension, which of course could change the present trend away from autarky and toward the opening of the Soviet economy.

2. Development Models of Industrial Cooperation

Slow increases in the number and scope of East-West industrial cooperation agreements can be expected. Because of the lack of a suitable collective institutional system and cooperation mechanism, the CMEA countries have so far been unable to benefit from the advantages arising from their great combined weight in their economic relations with Western Europe. In establishing cooperation relations the enterprises of the socialist countries have also kept primarily their own interests in view. This is related to the polycentric nature of CMEA planning cooperation. At the same time, their partners, the big multinational firms of Western Europe, are able to cooperate efficiently on the basis of their supranational nature, their possibilities of procuring state financing, their access to up-to-date information, and their diversification and financial strength.

Because of the existing differences in scale and financial strength between Eastern and Western enterprises, the bases for effective cooperation for the enterprises of the CMEA countries must be created in this decade by making production integration more intensive as well as by extending enterprise cooperation. These enterprises must strive to join in Soviet-Western industrial cooperation activities wherever possible, through contract work or in other ways. This will make possible profitable manufacturing production, mostly in large series. Within this overall strategy the individual countries must strive to locate possibilities for cooperation through which the Western firms can penetrate the whole CMEA market, because the Western partner takes part in industrial cooperation on a major scale primarily where such involvement is possible.

We can expect that cooperation agreements will be long-term and comprehensive, covering a range of questions from cooperation to the settlement of production and sales problems. On the basis of the favorable experience of the Soviet Union, it will be advisable — and it may be likely — that the other CMEA countries develop a conscious and purposeful strategy in East-West industrial cooperation and establish the necessary institutional framework for implementation of this policy. After the individual CMEA countries have developed detailed cooperation strategies, there might be a need to coordinate them within a CMEA framework in order to make possible a more effective stand.

East-West Cooperation

More rapid expansion of cooperation will also require Western companies to take the development priorities of the socialist countries increasingly into account. They will also have to stop blocking the growth of imports from the socialist countries and show greater readiness to cooperate on third country markets.

Thus it is in the interest of both the socialist and the Western countries to rapidly develop industrial cooperation. The goal on both sides is to seek opportunities for cooperation. However, in both the West and the socialist countries, we have now moved beyond the idea that cooperation relations should be considered a panacea solving the basic problems of East-West relations. It is obvious that first we must solve the structural and institutional problems.

The main problem with cooperation agreements with the West, at least on the Hungarian side, is that these projects are relatively small. This and other factors have created a vicious circle in forming cooperation agreements.

On the one hand, the trend of modern industrial development, marked by the spread of the multinational companies, forces us to strive to reach world levels of technical and scientific progress as soon as possible. This is necessary not only for economic growth but also to maintain the level of our foreign trade with the capitalist countries. The more we procrastinate in reaching this level, the greater the gap will be, and the more difficult it will be for us to increase our exports to the advanced industrial countries.

On the other hand, cooperation with the advanced industrialized countries through cooperation with the big international companies could lead to economic and technological dependence. There are substantial economic hazards inherent in development along such lines. We are thus forced to try to raise our technological standards through cooperation with small and medium-sized companies that are on the periphery of advanced technology. This too could lead to undesirable repercussions. But if we continue on our current path, our technological lag will continue to grow, and our balance of payments with Western countries will continue to deteriorate, which could again result in increased economic dependence on the capitalist countries.

In my opinion we must first recognize the limitations imposed by this vicious circle and then try to break out of it. I am convinced that the reason for inadequate development of Western industrial cooperation lies not so much in the political sensitivity of the subject as in the fact that we have not yet sufficiently considered the economic side of these questions. We are not prepared with the new proposals needed to influence the course of development. Our ideas on cooperation strategy and development, drawn up in the late sixties, are now outdated. We must adjust to new conditions and formulate a new strategy.

Potential CMEA strategies for East-West cooperation must be studied in two parts. First, let us consider the problem of the strategy of the CMEA countries, apart from the Soviet Union, in East-West cooperation.

There is still no common, coordinated strategy of any kind covering all the details of the development of East-West cooperation among the CMEA countries. In the short term it appears that enterprises in the CMEA countries, apart from the Soviet Union — which may establish cooperation relations on the Western European market — will continue to take into account basically only their own country. No collective institutional system has been created with the authority to adopt decisions and concentrate solely on the overall development of the CMEA countries in formulating a strategy for cooperation with Western Europe.

Thus I believe that the CMEA countries are not at present in a position to take collective advantage of the benefits of their great economic weight vis-à-vis Western Europe, particularly the Common Market. They could do so only through an institutional system of a collective nature.

In order to avoid any misunderstandings, I should particularly stress that the further development of economic and technological cooperation among the CMEA countries and their enterprises in the spirit of the Comprehensive Program plays a decisive role in the further development of the whole CMEA and the individual socialist countries. It follows that over the long term, the development of East-West cooperation must be based on the development of cooperation relations of the CMEA countries; but this does not exclude — indeed, to a certain extent it assumes — the maximum exploitation of bilateral relations with the West.

We have thus reached the point in our train of thought at which we can conclude, on the one hand, that the Hungarian cooperation strategy formulated at the end of the sixties needs to be reconsidered; on the other hand, in the main, the positions of the CMEA countries other than the Soviet Union are fundamentally tied to national considerations.

Hence it is of primary importance to assess the USSR's strategic objectives in participating in East-West industrial cooperation and the main potential areas for both industrial and enterprise cooperation. At the same time, they could also be areas to be considered by the smaller CMEA countries in formulating overall and sectoral strategies.

According to Soviet views there might be some change in the nature and direction of technological and scientific development in the socialist and Western European countries following the Conference on European Security. A great deal of high-level, basic research is being done in the socialist countries, and this could be suitably supplemented by Western European experimental and production facilities. Comprehensive business relations could be established and Western firms could provide major assistance in marketing, in which they have long traditions. It is the Soviet position that European-wide cooperation could eventually help solve the following common problems: the creation of new sources of energy and construction materials and improvement of existing ones; prospecting for and exploitation of mineral deposits and development of new types of substitute materials; ocean research, etc. There is also an increasingly strong need for the coordinated development in Europe of the scientific and technical infrastructure, the flow of scientific and technological information, patent matters, standardization, and measurement matters. Cooperation would

The Future of Socialist Economic Integration

also open up new possibilities for environmental protection.

According to Western sources models have been developed in recent years that will probably form the framework for long-term Soviet-Western cooperation. The most important of them is exploitation of Soviet sources of raw materials with Western technical and financial support. The Soviet Union will pay in raw materials for equipment and technical services provided on credit. Another form is the purchase by the USSR of turn-key projects from the West. In these cases the Western partner supplies parts for the finished products for a given time. In a later stage of production, the Western company receives some components from the Soviet plant for incorporation into its own products. There are more and more examples of the division of production based on the supply of parts abroad, particularly in the engineering industry. In all cases the market is divided. The Soviet partner supplies the socialist market, and the foreign partner, the Western market.

Last but not least, we mention joint ventures operating in the West, which have been set up mainly to promote the sale of Soviet products in the West. They are joint sales enterprises in which the Soviet foreign trade enterprise responsible for the sale of a product has joined forces with foreign agencies. The Soviet Union also takes part in joint production ventures in capitalist countries. They include the Scaldia (Volga) enterprise set up in Belgium to assemble and sell Soviet-made vehicles, oil refineries set up in Belgium and France, etc.

On the basis of our analysis of the Soviet Union's objectives for East-West cooperation, we can conclude that they are definite, purposeful, and cover all details. Hungary and the other small CMEA countries should formulate their strategies in a similar fashion.

We can conclude that because of the relatively limited national markets in the majority of CMEA countries, the major capitalist companies primarily show an interest in the CMEA market as a whole or in its biggest national market, the Soviet Union. They are only interested in the smaller national markets to the extent that they satisfy the special economic and technological requirements of a given undertaking, or to the extent that they are able to penetrate the CMEA market through cooperation agreements in these smaller markets or to import important raw materials.

It is thus very probable that as in the Zhiguli program, the smaller socialist countries can only benefit from many undertakings on a larger scale if they take part in cooperation between the Soviet Union and the advanced capitalist countries.

The following are examples of possible cooperation schemes:

a. Delivery of parts which are sent to plants set up in the Soviet Union under the direction of a Western firm, and which are produced on the basis of technological documentation provided by the Soviet partner or directly by the capitalist partner. This is the scheme used in Zhiguli cooperation.

b. Purchase of licenses and know-how coordinated with the Soviet Union, on the basis of which on the one hand we supply the Soviet Union, and on the other hand we can cover the convertible currency costs of buying the license by making counterdeliveries to the capitalist companies granting the license.

c. Organization of joint foreign trade offices for given types of products, for example, for the products produced under coordinated license purchases that could be marketed jointly.

d. The following scheme is similar to that used in the development of Hungarian motor vehicle production. In this scheme we develop a product — such as buses — oriented toward the entire CMEA market, which we then also export to the capitalist countries to counterbalance convertible currency costs incurred to achieve world market quality, control, and technological standards. This can also be done in cooperation with the Soviet Union and the other CMEA countries.

e. Another scheme: large-scale credit and investment deals in which the purpose is not only the transfer of technology and know-how but also the involvement of capital. It is conceivable that a small socialist country like Hungary could manufacture and deliver parts, components, and finished products on such a scale that it could also supply the product to the socialist market. This case is the opposite of "d," because in this case

The Future of Socialist Economic Integration

cooperation begins with large-scale capitalist cooperation that leads to supplying the socialist market with world standard, high-quality products at world market prices.

f. Apart from the Soviet Union there are also possibilities for joining in large-scale capitalist cooperation development plans with other CMEA countries. In particular the example of Poland in connection with Fiat and other cooperation projects should be mentioned.

g. Finally, there are medium- and small-scale production cooperation projects with small and medium-sized enterprises. They must continue to hold an important place in our cooperation strategies. Since we are a small country, we must also strive to satisfy the special needs of small market segments taking advantage of the flexibility of our economic system. Diversification increases our security and can be achieved, among other ways, by satisfying the special demands of neglected customer groups, using modern methods of marketing, and concentrating on good customer service, punctual deliveries, and high quality.

3. Questions of Long-term Planning of East-West Cooperation

Long-term planning has an ever greater influence on East-West economic relations. Since both the socialist and the Western countries expect these relations to continue to expand, it is understandable that they are striving to establish policies and goals for a longer period.

The European socialist countries quite clearly have an interest in the extension of economic relations with the Western countries. This is expressed in the fact that they count on the development of East-West economic relations when engaging in economic planning and incorporate them into their long-term economic development plans.

In the course of cooperation each country must independently decide on the areas and questions for which it wants to coordinate and jointly plan economic development policy in the context of cooperation. Naturally coordination of the different elements of the countries' economic policy in East-West economic relations can only progress to the extent that the partners attempt coordination on the basis of their interests.

We cannot yet speak of the coordination of economic policies in East-West economic relations. Obviously progress in this area can only come slowly and gradually, and in the coming years cooperation will be primarily confined to simple forms.

In the following I would like to shed some light on the issue of long-term planning of East-West cooperation. In doing so I am naturally aware that the problems of planning foreign trade with the capitalist world and the success and problems of such trade are well known in both the East and the West. However, in my opinion East-West cooperation also calls for a new theoretical and practical approach to long-term planning. The following considerations arise in this context.

It is now recognized in both the East and West that East-West cooperation projects can only play a role in economic growth, the development of the economy, and mutual trade if they can be incorporated into the long-term plans of the socialist countries. The reason is that processes which develop slowly, but have a great effect, play a large role in the development of the national economies. Certain elements of these processes depend on cooperation projects that usually have long gestation periods. Obviously we cannot plan major changes in the economy related to cooperation projects within the framework of a five-year plan. Essential changes can only take place over a much longer period. Cooperation projects in sectors that need long-term development can be put into operation on the basis of ten- or fifteen-year technical and economic plans. The increased use of the elements of long-term planning is therefore a necessity on both sides.

East-West cooperation projects of general significance can be used in the planning work of the socialist countries only if they are based on coordinated plans and comprehensive, long-term macroeconomic and external economic considerations.

Lacking this they do not provide a sound planning basis for the formulation of five-year plans. Only in this way can they be incorporated into the development of production integration among the CMEA countries.

The requirement of long-term planning of East-West cooperation projects also definitely calls for the satisfaction of a number of demands arising in connection with several as yet unsolved problems. One is that alternatives should be drawn up on the national economic level to select possible large-scale cooperation projects. They should contain mainly possible alternatives for standards, conditions, and efficiency parameters and should also include mutual information. Because of rapid changes in technology and the large risk involved in cooperation measures substantially influencing the development of the national economy, it is of vital importance to draw up these alternative proposals.

We can conclude that the economic processes related to developments in East-West cooperation incorporate many uncertainties over the long term. They appear not only in the external environment but also within the internal goals of the East-West cooperation agreements. In my opinion, therefore, cooperation projects, plans, and agreements embodying short-term, direct action programs should be made realistic on both sides — and above all by the socialist countries — by providing for reserves to eliminate the disruptive effects of uncertainties.

I have in mind here not only that data on supplies of materials and technical expertise and financial resources be included as reserves in the shorter-term economic plans in order to take advantage of opportunities that could arise from East-West cooperation. I believe the question is rather the extent to which the implementation of cooperation in harmony with the strengthening of the long-term approach contributes to achieving equilibrium and supports the reality of the plan for the national economy.

Another idea in this context is that the plan should be flexible with regard to requirements of the cooperation agreements that are likely to change. More realistic planning in this area would mainly be ensured by formulating both more and less ambitious alternatives. They should objectively state the assumptions on which East-West cooperation projects rest and the consequences of their acceptance.

The planning of East-West cooperation cannot be limited to macroeconomic processes because policies for the various economic sectors are also very important for the plan. Of basic importance here are the time needed for development of cooperation and the expected duration of the most important effects of the decisions. Planning must be centered largely on processes of long duration. We can expect that the planning requirements for the creation of a European transport network, a united European energy system, and the like can be discussed with a time horizon of several decades; in such cases planning in preparation for quantitative decisions plays a greater role. Elsewhere, where the primary factor is the speed of technological and market changes, it is not primarily the quantitative guidelines but rather scientific, technical, and other economic policy developments influencing development that have to be forecasted.

The development of European-wide cooperation calls for a whole series of practical regulations in terms of relations between the two regions. They include solving the problem of long-term planning. Experience to date clearly demonstrates that only a practical approach is successful. An important element in such an approach is the problem of sharing risks and gains. It is an aspect affecting both East-West and CMEA cooperation. It is therefore appropriate to examine it separately.

4. Risk and Risk Sharing in Cooperation

For the capitalist partner the main element of risk in cooperation with CMEA countries is presumably that state intervention in enterprise matters and in other affairs (e.g., price policy) can be arbitrary and unpredictable.

In the case of Hungary the Western firms' major risks can

be characterized as follows:

— the size of the Hungarian market, including the effects of state intervention in the market;

— sales opportunities on the markets of other socialist countries (if they were originally anticipated);

— changes in the market that affect the partner firm and are likely to impair its "performance" for the capitalist partner;

— state intervention in the dealings of the Hungarian partner having the same effect;

— changes in the sovereign development and business policies of the Hungarian firm that are unfavorable for the capitalist partner.

In cooperation the first three factors are most significant, while in the case of joint ventures in Hungary, the last is most important. A separate problem is that in joint ventures, the relatively weak financial position of the Hungarian firms in terms of their own assets can produce mistrust. It is well known that large enterprises in particular are in a weak position in this respect. They can get money for important ventures only through state preferential funds. The question is whether in the preliminary but highly important state of negotiations on cooperation the capitalist partners can be expected to believe that these preferences will be given. In general the position of Hungarian small and medium-sized enterprises is better in this respect, and their financial autonomy is relatively greater. But they can be expected to undertake only small-volume cooperation projects.

5. Conclusions

Differences in concepts of European-wide cooperation are not found only in the capitalist countries of Wester Europe. The different theories existing in the economic literature of the socialist countries, in their practical economic policies, and in the concepts of instruments of economic control have not been fully clarified nor are they unequivocal. What has come to the fore and is growing increasingly strong is the concept that international trade is an important factor of growth, and that it is vital for efficient economic development to take advantage of the benefits inherent in the international division of labor and to achieve extensive economic cooperation. However, it is understandable that time is needed to clarify ideas and to switch from one theory to another. On the one hand — largely on the basis of past experience — the view is sometimes expressed in the socialist countries that it is not possible to rely on the stability of economic relations with the advanced capitalist countries. Such a view assumes that the interest of these countries might suddenly decline with a change in the market situation, which could disturb the course of East-West trade. However, in my opinion we can also see a lack of conceptual clarity arising from difficulties in the extension of relations and the novelty of production integration, and this should be taken into consideration. In particular, I have in mind the problems of the small countries, especially in terms of investment. It has therefore been my intention to study this aspect in the light of Hungarian experience.

The main problem from the enterprise standpoint in industrial cooperation agreements with the advanced Western European countries is that these agreements are relatively small in volume, both individually and as a whole. With the present state of economic control methods, this mainly arises from the fact that as a result of the decisions already made in development policy investment allocations, the state does not have the resources to emphasize such cooperation projects.

We also tried to see how advisable it is for Hungary to organize joint ventures with Western firms, and to what extent our financial regulations have created a favorable atmosphere for attracting foreign capital. I am aware that views on this question differ in Hungary.

According to some opinions our measures so far have been inadequate, ambiguous, and hesitant. Thus it can hardly be expected that foreign funds will be invested in joint ventures. However, according to others the existing rules are already excessive, and there is basically no need to invite foreign capital.

These two extreme positions show that the subject is politically sensitive on the one hand and yet inadequately clarified economically on the other. This lack of clear concepts is primarily due to the fact that we do not yet have our own practical experiences in this regard, nor do we possess an overall strategy. This is even truer if we consider the question in terms of CMEA production integration.

We have considered the enterprise management, trade, taxation problems, and experiences related to foreign investments. We have studied and evaluated Hungarian financial regulations against this background. Our conclusions are, so far, that Hungarian joint ventures have been set up with capitalist companies not to attract capital but to import technology and know-how in cases in which we have been unable to secure these imports successfully in some other way. It can be assumed that the situation is similar in other CMEA countries. The related consequences for the development of production integration among the CMEA countries must therefore be considered.

I should mention in this respect that imports of technology undoubtedly occupy an important place in the foreign trade of the socialist countries and in Hungary's foreign trade priorities. However, to make it the sole objective would severely limit the area of economic relations with the capitalist countries. It forces the role of East-West trade into the background to a certain extent and also reduces the importance of considerations that arise from comparative advantage and from efforts to raise technical standards. For this reason the view that solely stresses the importance of technology imports is a one-sided concept of East-West trade. However, the situation is changing: the involvement of capital may become an important new objective.

The characteristic feature of joint ventures — the chief objective being not to attract investment but primarily to import technology and know-how — engenders the following problems in addition to those already mentioned.

The foreign partner has an intensive interest in the modernity and high quality of technology exports if it has a large share in the joint venture or undertaking. However, if these high-share participations in technology are small in volume, this quantitative limitation permits technology imports of only relatively minor importance. This situation is thus not likely to permit important technology imports for the national economy, which would have a decisive structural influence.

On the other hand, arranging for relatively minor capital and technology imports through Hungarian joint ventures could also spontaneously lead to a situation in which we could count mainly on the interest of smaller and medium-sized capitalist firms within the framework of these investment possibilities. Small investments hardly make it worthwhile for big companies to carry out the necessary organizational work (unless they use the small undertakings as a springboard to penetrate a market). Moreover substantial problems from the national economic point of view are involved in such cooperation with big companies, especially with multinational enterprises.

Taking into account approximately the same level of risk for the Hungarian and foreign partner in joint undertakings, it is generally small and medium-sized companies that would make desirable partners for our enterprises. For these reasons we should emphasize small and medium-sized capitalist companies in seeking to acquire foreign partners. However, the joint ventures that could be created in this way would be largely of micro- rather than macroeconomic importance. And this would not ensure the exploitation of major opportunities.

A new plan of action is possible if the attraction of capital can also be adopted as a goal in cooperation with the West. In this case the creation of production relations with major international enterprises prompts the reconsideration of all our financial regulations and the rethinking of our strategy.

We have again reached the conclusion that the small countries of the CMEA face a new situation. The expansion of CMEA integration presents new possibilities, and the exploration and use of these opportunities as soon as possible adds a new dimension to the process of integration itself.

Notes

Notes to Chapter 2

1. A detailed review and rich bibliography on this subject is contained in Pál Kállai, Nemzetközi ipari kooperáció, Budapest, Közgazdasagi es Jogi Könyvkiadó, 1971.
2. Nowe Drogi (Warsaw), January 1970, p. 94; Ekonomická Revue, Prague, June 1968, p. 310.
3. In this context a new problem arises. If the curtailment of production is not coordinated, the production of machinery needed for still existing production will also cease in the CMEA countries. Today it is paradoxically true that obsolete and outdated machines that once were "soft" are becoming "hard" because everyone has refrained from producing them, although they are still needed to maintain production. Every country has now begun to produce them again. Thus the need for coordination is evident here as well: that is, decisions cannot be made unilaterally. This way of developing production demands communication.
4. This seems to be so primarily on account of the given price policy preferences in the given price systems.

Notes to Chapter 3

1. A. N. Bikov, Nauchno-tekhnicheskaia integratsiia sotsialisticheskikh stran, Moscow, "Nauka" Publishers, 1974, p. 36.
2. Aussenwirtschaft, 1975, no. 19.
3. Eastern Europe Report, Business International, 1976, no. 23.

Notes

Note to Chapter 4

1. For a detailed discussion of sovereignty and integration, see Tibor Kiss, <u>Nemzetközi munkamegosztás és Magyarország gazdasági növekedése</u>, Budapest, Kossuth Könyvkiadó, 1969, pp. 140-47.

Notes to Chapter 5

1. For details, see, János Szita, "A KGST XXIX. budapesti ülésszakáról," <u>Gazdaság</u>, 1975, no. 3, p. 93, and N. V. Bautina, ed., <u>Sotrudnichestvo stran SEV v oblasti planovoi deiatel'nosti</u>, Moscow, "Mysl'" Publishers, 1975, pp. 37-39.
2. Regional aspects of location are discussed in detail in the next chapter.
3. See the declaration by Ádám Juhász, secretary for heavy industry, on the building of the Orenburg pipeline, <u>Világgazdaság</u>, July 6, 1976.
4. Tibor Kiss, op. cit., pp. 73-74.
5. Speech by Lubomir Strougal at the Thirtieth Session of the CMEA, Uj szó, July 9, 1976.
6. This was stated in other terms but in a similar way by N. V. Bautina: "The system of national economic planning entails all the forces of production of society, including those that are of international importance. Precisely on this account, national planning is the starting point for all forms of joint planning activity" ("K voprosu metodologii sovmestnoi planovoi deiatel'nosti," <u>Izvestiia Akademii nauk SSSR, Seriia ekonomicheskaia</u>, 1974, no. 5).
7. S. M. Sorokin, <u>Problemy vosproizvodstva i planirovaniia sotsialisticheskoi ekonomiki</u>, Moscow, "Nauka" Publishers, 1976.
8. For a detailed analysis of industrial structure policy in the GDR, see Erich Honecker, "Zu aktuelle Fragen bei der Verwirkliching des Beschlusses unseres VIII, Parteitages," <u>Neues Deutschland</u>, December 18, 1971.

Notes to Chapter 6

1. This subject is discussed in detail in I. M. Maiergol'ts and V. P. Maiakovskii, eds., <u>Problemy ekonomicheskoi geografii zarubezhnoi sotsialisticheskoi Evropi</u>, Moscow, "Mysl'" Publishers, 1974.
2. By present-valuing the investment contribution and adding the Soviet export price, one can work out what other kind of imports can still compete with the Siberian import price.
3. Investment needs of the integration export development projects must be calculated by including the necessary subsequent investments (approximating the latter using input-output tables). The per unit investment requirement reached thus may be much greater than the normal one in international practice in general; investments are usually made in areas that al-

Notes

ready have an infrastructure. (In practice the subsequent investments are not always worked out by means of the input-output methods, but the investment contribution asked for is high in itself.)

Notes to Chapter 7

1. The Comprehensive Program of the CMEA (Hungarian version), Budapest, Kossuth Könyvkiadó, 1971, p. 8.
2. A detailed analysis of the accounting system and the monetary relations is found in Kálmán Pécsi, "Megjegyzések a szocialista nemzetközi pénzügyi rendszer történetéhez," Közgazdasági Szemle, 1976, no. 1, and Imre Vincze, A KGST nemzetközi elszámolási rendszere, Budapest, Közgazdasági és Jogi Könyvkiadó, 1978.
3. K. Pécsi, "Nekotorye problemy ustanovleniia tsen vo vzaimnoi torgovle," Tribuna ekonomista i mezhdunarodnika, 1979, no. 9.
4. Let me quote some economists holding this view: "For products supplied under specialization and cooperation agreements, the pricing principle previously adopted for the CMEA market is still valid. These products are sold at prices determined by taking into account the price basis of the world's commodity markets, which do not sufficiently take into account the special features of cooperation. For example, machine parts are two to three times the price of the same parts if they are installed in the finished machine.

"The prices of parts and components, if stated on the basis of the prices of similar products on the world market but supplied in the framework of cooperation, may become disadvantageous for the cooperating partner.

"Obviously, in such cases exceptions must be made to the general rules of trade transacted at world market prices. The legal basis for this was created by the Twenty-third Session of the CMEA (that is, the possibility of deviating from contractual prices established on a world market price basis in economically justified cases). It seems that in cases in which the world market prices do not provide mutual advantages for those participating in the exchange, it is expedient to set prices at a level at which efficiency of cooperation is assured" (N. V. Bautina and V. M. Shastitko, "Ispol'zovanie tovarno-denezhnykh instrumentov v protsesse sovmestnoi planovoi deiatel'nosti," in Sotrudnitchestvo stran-chlenov SEV v oblasti planovoi deiatel'nosti, pp. 126-27).
5. Ibid., p. 127.
6. Világgazdaság, June 1976.
7. See I. Motorin, Kriterii effektivnosti v sisteme upravleniia vneshneekonomicheskimi sviazami, Aktual'nye problemy sotsialisticheskoi ekonomicheskoi integratsii stran-chlenov SEV, Moscow, CMEA Institute, 1972, p. 287.
8. I. Motorin, "Metodologicheskie problemy dolgosrochnogo planirovaniia integratsionnykh protsessov," Planovoe khoziaistvo, 1975, no. 2.

Notes

Notes to Chapter 8

1. László Csaba, "Az integració és a gazdasági mechanizmus összefüggése a Közép-Keleteurópai szocialista országokban" (dissertation), January 1978, Archives of the Research Institute for World Economy, pp. 109-12.
2. Petr Chvojka, "Monetary Relations in the Development of International Socialist Integration. An Attempt at Exploring Their Present Rules," Politická Ekonomie, 1976, no. 6.
3. George Crainiceanu, "Role of the National Currency in Foreign Trade and the Consequences of Convertibility," Era Socialista, 1977, no. 12.
4. In addition, direct reexports and reimports transacted with the mediation of third firms have to be taken into account. Since they are not caught in the statistics, they have been neglected here.
5. Since 1971 the Statistical Yearbook of Hungary shows foreign trade both by groups of countries and by groups of currencies.
6. Paul Marer, East European Economies Post-Helsinki, August 25, 1977, p. 565; Josef M. van Brabant, East European Cooperation: The Role of Money and Finance, New York, Praeger, 1977, pp. 353-54.
7. Külkereskedelmi Statisztikaiév könyv, 1978.
8. Eight percent of the trade transacted with the socialist countries, or 10% of the trade accounted in rubles.
9. It has been published in the press, and it is known from the international economic literature, that crude oil was exchanged for grain and meat; that because of the Common Market embargo on meat, the USSR bought meat for convertible foreign exchange, etc.
10. Klára Beke and László Hunyadi, "A magyar export importanyag tartalma," Külgazdasag, 1977, no. 7. The article is based on a joint publication of the Economic Department, Ministry of Foreign Trade, and the Econometric Department of the Research Institute for Computer Techniques. The computations were performed by F. Tibor Liska with the ICL System 4/70 computer of the Computer Center of the National Planning Office. Important research was done on the subject by György Szakolczai.
11. The data come from the Central Statistical Office for 1978. These figures show the trade and transport costs settled between the socialist and, within them, between the CMEA countries in convertible foreign exchange. For some socialist countries all trade is settled in currencies other than the ruble (e.g., Yugoslavia, Cuba until 1976, China since 1977).
12. They appear as money (means of accounting and payment) in such credit agreements between member countries or between the common banks and their clients, as well as in commodity trade settlements, when credit is granted in convertible currency and must be repaid in the same currency, and when the balance of the commodity supplies accounted in convertible currency must be settled at least in principle in such currency. They appear, however, as special commodities when the amount in convertible currency is converted to transferable rubles. This occurs typically with investment contributions when the convertible foreign exchange is a part of the total contri-

Notes

bution; it is credited to the contributing country in transferable rubles, and it is repaid in transferable rubles. On the other hand, it occurs in indirect trade settled in convertible currencies when parts, machines, units, etc., imported from the West are built in and exported to socialist countries. Obviously, in such cases the "price"of the special commodity — that is, the rate of exchange of the convertible currency against the transferable ruble — becomes particularly important.

13. We know that the exchange of the transferable ruble is possible today in practice only if it is closely related to the flow of commodities, and also that credits granted in transferable rubles that have no direct cover in convertible foreign exchange only amount to a regrouping of assets within the community and not to additional assets.

14. László Csaba, "Az ár és a hatékonyság összefüggései a szocialista kereskedelemben" (report), Archives of the Institute for World Economy, Budapest, 1976.

15. To make the idea clear, I would like to cite only two examples. The first relates to soft sawnwood and apples. We know that the former is a hard good, while the latter is the softest article in CMEA trade. Annually we export about 280,000 tons of apples to the Soviet Union. To make the necessary packaging material, we import 200,000 cubic meters of soft sawnwood. (150,000 cu m are used for the cases, and 50,000 cu m are waste.) We then reexport the cases to the USSR. (See Magyar Nemzet, May 7, 1978, p. 7.) In addition the export of apples requires fuel, heavy machine tools imported from socialist countries, and fertilizers, insecticides, light machines and hand tools, etc., imported for convertible currencies. The soft sawnwood is a hard commodity because it is a raw material, while apples are soft commodities because they are traded as a residual.

The other example relates to cotton, wool, and carpets. The first two are hard, while the latter is soft. The direct import content of carpet production is 70%, of which 10% comes from socialist and 60% from Western countries.

Notes to Chapter 9

1. According to the formulation of András Simon, all programs can be considered optimal which have the property that the objective function of no country can be increased without reducing the value of the objective function of another country. See András Simon, "Nemzetközi optimumszámítási model összeállításának problemai," Külgazdasag, 1972, no. 11, and András Simon, "Több ország gazdaság optimalizálásának problémái" (doctoral dissertation).

2. In A. S. Tolkachev, ed., A társadalmi hatékonyság kerdései, Budapest, Közgazdasági es Jogi Könyvkiadó, 1975, p. 288.

3. I. Motorin, "A külgazdasági kapcsolatok különböző formáinak összhangja," in ibid., p. 307.

4. Ibid.

Notes

5. Pál Vallus, "A termelés anyagigényessége," <u>Figyelő</u>, June 9, 1976.

Notes to Chapter 10

1. This is reflected in the resolution by the Central Committee of the Hungarian Socialist Workers' Party (October 1977) on long-term foreign trade policy and the development of the production structure, as well as by its December 1978 resolution on national economic equilibrium.

2. The outlined effect of Soviet-Western trade can also have a psychological impact on production integration, which must not be underestimated. For example, in Moscow a laundry in one district is equipped with American machinery, while in another there are machines from CMEA member countries. In the first shop there are long lines; in the other there are none, mainly because of quality differences between the two kinds of service. A more open economy and less autarky can involve serious consequences in production integration and will promote higher quality standards.

Bibliography

"Activités futures de la C. E. E. dans le domaine de la cooperation industrielle," Comission Economique pour l'Europe, Coop. ind., February 24, 1972.

Ausch, Sandor, A KGST-együttműködés helyzete, mechanizmus, távlatai, Budapest, Közgazdasági es Jogi Könyvkiadó, 1969.

―――――, Theory and Practice of CMEA Cooperation, Budapest, Akadémia Kiadó, 1969.

Bautina, N. V., "K voprosu metodologii sovmestnoi planovoi deiatel'nosti," Izvestiia Akademii nauk SSSR, 1974, no. 5.

Bautina, N. V., ed., Sotrudnitchestvo stran-chlenov SEV v oblasti planovoi deiatel'nosti, Moscow, "Mysl'" Publishers, 1975.

Bikov, A. N., Nauchno-tekhnicheskaia integratsiia sotsialisticheskikh stran, Moscow, "Nauka" Publishers, 1974.

Brabant, J. M. von, "Specialization and Import Dependence of Some East European Countries," Jahrbuch der Wirtschaft Osteuropas, vol. 5, Munich, 1974.

Csikos-Nagy, Béla, Socialist Price Theory and Price Policy, Budapest, Akadémia Kiadó, 1975.

Drabowski, E., "Problemy wymenalnosci walut Krajów RWPG," Handel Zagraniczny, 1974, no. 2.

Farkas, György, "A külföldivel közös hazai társulások, a külföldi beruházások és a kooperációk néhány pénzügyi kérdése Magyarországon," Gazdaság es Jogtudomany, 1974, no. 2.

Fekete, János, "Monetary Crisis and Socialist Economy," in The Hungarian Economy, 1974.

Friedman, W. G., "The Contractual Joint Venture," Columbia Journal of

Bibliography

World Business, 1972, no. 1.

Johnson, Harry, Direct Foreign Investment: A Survey of the Issues, Sydney, 1970.

Káplár, József, Munkamegosztás a szocialista világgazdaságban, Budapest, Kossuth Könyvkiadó, 1969.

Kerékgyártó, György, A KGST-országok tudományosmuszaki együttműködése, Budapest, Kossuth Könyvkiadó, 1974.

Kiss, Tibor, Nemzetközi munkamegosztás és Magyarország gazdasági növekedése, Budapest, Kossuth Könyvkiadó, 1969.

Kozma, Ferenc, "Gondolatok a szocialista integráció továbbfejlesztéséről," Gazdaság, 1974, no. 3.

Köves, András, "Gazdasági kapcsolatok a Szovjetunió és a fejlett tőkésországok közöh" (dissertation), Budapest, 1975.

Lenin, V. I., "A szocialista forradalom és a nemzetek önrendelkezési joga," Lenin Összes Művei, vol. 27, Budapest, Kossuth Könyvkiadó, 1971.

Maiergol'ts, I. M., and Maiakovskii, V. P., eds., Problemy ekonomicheskoi geografii zarubezhnoi sotsialisticheskoi Evropy, Moscow, "Mysl'" Publishers, 1974.

Meissner, H., "Der Beitrag der Multinationalen Unternehmungen zur Entwicklung der Weltwirtschaft," Kyklos, vol. 25, 1972, no. 3.

Meizel, Sándor, Mit kell tudni a KGST-ról?, Budapest, Kossuth Könyvkiadó, 1974.

Mervart, J., Cilové Programové Plánováni v metodologii praci na dlouhodobem vyhledu, Prague, Vyzkumny Ustav Planovani a rizeni narodniho hospodarstvi, 1974.

Motorin, I., "Kriterii effektivnosti v sisteme upravleniia vneshne-ekonomicheskimi sviaziami," Aktual'nye problemy sotsialisticheskoi ekonomicheskoi integratsii stran-chlenov SEV, Moscow, CMEA Institute, 1972.

————, "Metodologicheskie problemy dolgosrochnogo planirovaniia integratsionnykh protsessov," Planovoe khoziaistvo, 1975, no. 2.

Nemes, Ferenc, and Roth, András, "A gépipar termelés szakosításának néhány kérdése," Gazdaság, 1975, no. 4.

Nyers, Rezső, "A fokozatos konvertabilitásra vonatkozó magyar javaslat," Külkereskedelem, February 1969.

Palánkai, Tibor, Nemzetközi gazdasági integráció, Korunk világgazdasága, vol. 1, Budapest, Közgazdasági es Jogi Könyvkiadó, 1973.

Páldi, András, A gazdaságirányítas és tervezés reformja a Szovjetunióban, Budapest, Kossuth Könyvkiadó, 1976.

Pavlov, Iu. M., Regional'nye problemy ekonomicheskoi integratsii SSSR v sisteme stran SEV, Moscow, "Nauka" Publishers, 1975.

Pécsi, Kálmán, "A beruházási együttműködés néhány nemzetközi pénzügyi vonatkozása a KGST országokban," Közgazdasági Szemle, 1964, no. 2.

————, "Megjegyzések a szocialista nemzetközi pénzügyi rendszer történetéhez," Közgazdasági Szemle, 1964, no. 4.

————, "Some Aspects of Long-Term Planning in the East-West Cooperation," in Perspektiven und Probleme wirtschaftlicher Zusammen-

Bibliography

arbeit zwischen Ost und Westeuropa, Humboldt and Berlin, Deutsches Institut fur Wirtschaftsforschung, Sonderheft 114, 1976.

―――――, Teoreticheskie problemy valutno-kreditnykh otnoshenii v mirovoi sotsialisticheskoi sisteme, Moscow, "Mir" Publishers, 1974.

Shiriaev, Iu. S., A szocialista integráció gazdasági mechanizmusa, Budapest, Kossuth Könyvkiadó and Közgazdasági és Jogi Könyvkiadó, 1975.

Siman, Miklós, and Varga, György, "Adalékok a termelési szerkezet átalakításának szelektív módszeréhez," Gazdaság, 1976, no. 2.

Simon, András, "Nemzetközi optimumszámitási modell összéállításának problemai," Külgazdaság, 1972, no. 11.

Sivák, József and Vági, Ferencné, "A társadalmi termelés hatékonyságának mérése es tervezése," Közgazdasagi Szemle, 1976, no. 4.

Sonin, M. V., Szocialista integráció, Budapest, Közgazdasági és Jogi Könyvkiadó, 1975.

Sorokin, G. M., Problemy vosproizvodstva i planirovaniia sotsialisticheskoi ekonomiki, Moscow, "Nauka" Publishers, 1976.

Szelecki, György, "A gépipari szocialista nemzetközi együttműködés továbbfejlesztésének csomóponti kérdései" (doctoral dissertation), Budapest, 1975.

Szita, Janos, "A KGST XXIX ulésszakáról," Gazdaság, 1976, no. 3.

Tolkachev, A. S., ed., A társadalmi termelés hatékonysági kérdései, Budapest, Közgazdasági es Jogi Könyvkiadó, 1975.

Vajda, Imre, "Integráció, gazdasági unió és nemzeti állam," Közgazdasági Szemle, 1968, no. 4.

Vallus, Pál, "A termelés anyagigényessége," Figyelő, June 9, 1976.

Vernon, R., "Influence of National Origins on the Strategy of Multinational Enterprises," Revue Economique, 1972, no. 4.

About the Author

Kálmán Pécsi has served in a number of capacities in the organizations of socialist economic cooperation and integration and has long followed those bodies activities in his scholarly writings. He is the author of more than sixty articles in the field, as well as three books on CMEA relations published in Hungarian.

Professor Pécsi's work with CMEA organs includes a stint from 1964 to 1967 as a councillor in the Monetary and Financial Department of the Council and his current post as Chief of Department of Monetary and Commodity Relations of the CMEA Research Institute in Moscow. From 1956 to 1970 he was a section leader in the International Department of the Hungarian Ministry of Finances, concerned mainly with foreign exchange and balance-of-payments problems. At the Institute of Economic Planning of the Hungarian National Planning Office, Professor Pécsi has worked on theoretical and practical issues in CMEA specialization and cooperation (head of section since 1974). Finally, the author previously held the position of Head of Department on the Socialist Countries at the Institute of World Economics of the Hungarian Academy of Sciences in Budapest.